Dating with DIGNITY

THE SINGLE WOMAN'S GUIDE TO SUSTAINING *His* STANDARDS

Cesly Burgess

For information contact:
C. Burgess
P.O. Box 360657
2724 Wesley Chapel Rd.
Decatur, GA 30034
CeslyBurgess.com

Book and Cover design by TKO Photographic Graphic
ISBN: 978-0-692-16496-9

First Edition: August 2018

Dedication

Before all else, I dedicate this book to the one who put it in my heart in the first place, God!

To my supportive parents Jackie White & Lonzie Burgess, I love you both and am eternally grateful for the faith that you've always had in my ability to achieve everything I have aimed for.

To my grandparents John & Fannie White, and Cammie Mae Bellinger-Johnson thank you for defying the odds so that we all had a chance to do the same.

To my tribe...words cannot explain how much I adore and appreciate your endless support. When I wanted to stop, you kept me going and when I felt like I couldn't, you reminded me that I should and would! I couldn't ask for better friends.

ACKNOWLEDGEMENTS (OF SOME SORT)

If my synopsis didn't reveal this to you, I guess I should before you dive in: I'm not here to follow the classic literary structure of how things should be done and thus, these acknowledgments will be as non-traditional as the rest of the book.

Before anything, I want to thank God for giving me the vision and discontentment that led to the book in your hands. I thank Him for every bad relationship and or situationship, that I and my friends have ever experienced that led to what was shared in these pages. I thank Him for the wisdom to learn from my decisions that didn't lead to my greatest moments and the ones that have. I'm beyond grateful to have walked out this life in my shoes — the steps have strengthened me.

Who would I be without my parents? Mommy (yep, I still call her Mommy), I thank you for always believing in me no matter how little I believed in myself. From the second I told you about the book, I barely explained what it was about before you said "I can't wait to read it!" You're my favorite girl, my numero uno fan, and I couldn't imagine life without you. Thank you for everything.

Daddy, thank you for being open to me sharing our story. It wasn't always butterflies and roses, but it was the path that we needed to take to get us where we needed to go, in order to become who we were each destined to be. What was meant for my harm, God used for my good. Thank you for being the best father you knew how and for always pushing me to trust God at every turn.

I have way too many friends and family members to thank — but you know exactly who you are. Thank you for seeing my greatness before I did. I'm forever grateful for how you challenged me to be the best version of myself possible while celebrating who I unapologetically am. Your support, love, uplifting words, faith, and prayers were and are priceless to me. Kobe, Jordan, and Jayla — I hope I made the three of you proud to call me your sister. And to all of my single ladies, this one's for you. Thank you for hearing me, receiving my love, and trusting God. You were fearfully and wonderfully made from the day that you were born — never doubt that again.

To anyone who doesn't feel represented in the groups listed above: I adore and thank you for reading. You're literally holding a labor of love — and man are you in for a treat. There are a lot of interesting stories in between these covers...Enjoy!

PROLOGUE

You're single, SO WHAT?!

IF SOMEONE WOULD, PLEASE specify for me the day and time when being single was deemed a terminal illness, then I think I would finally understand. I would eventually comprehend why we're bombarded with dating shows, apps, blogs and books that tell us to raise our standards — while begging us to lower our expectations. It would then make sense as to why statistics aren't ever in our favor and telling us that once we hit a certain age, "it ain't happenin." We, as a single collective, would also unveil the truth as to why every inch of society is watching our biological clocks with such concern; as if our Abraham and Sarah bred Isaac would be any of their responsibility. Well, hear me all who have ears and please hear me clearly when I say, I, Cesly Burgess, am single — SO! WHAT!

Being single doesn't make me less than; it does not determine my level of self-esteem, and it will never give you the right to try and estimate my worth. In fact, being single means, I am more than a woman; I am a bold and beautiful Queen running her own castle.

Being single shows that my self-worth is not to be negotiated just to have a warm body in my bed. Most of all, being single reveals that I am more priceless than many can comprehend because if they truly understood the value of my heart they wouldn't be so hasty to tell me to give it away to someone who is less than the best.

So, to every assumption and every derogatory statement, to all who feel like my life is over if a wedding ring doesn't adorn my left hand before the following year, I have only one reply. Yes, I am single and I love it...so what?

Do you dare to declare the same? If not, save us both time and stop reading now, because the goal of this book isn't to teach you how to find a man. I'm not here to outline ten steps to a picture-perfect relationship. Instead, I am here to show you why you should throw society's caution flags to the wind and live your life!

Who am I to give this kind of advice? Your Single Life Liaison, allowing you to learn from my mistakes and thrive without the unnecessary growing pains. I've been in your shoes. I've had premarital sex, I've dated everyone from the drug dealer to the minister, and I am sitting here single and proud of it. No, I won't recant all of those stories for you, that's an entirely separate book in itself, haha! Yet, there is nothing better than sharing the truth with women who need to hear it. We are disciples, not just of the gospel, but of the love of Christ. I would be remiss if I didn't use my testimony to help you through your tests. And with that in mind, I ask that you grab a journal or write notes directly in the book, as we dive right into it — because by the end of this book not only will you see how priceless you are and the kind of man you deserve, but you'll also learn how to embrace your singleness while Dating with Dignity.

CONTENTS

CHAPTER 1

Put Your Crown Back On

I N THE INTRODUCTION, I said you'd be screaming "say it loud — I'm single and proud!" This is not because of some psychological mind trick or because I'm going to guilt you into these words. No, I would never use trickery to crown a Queen, since it's truly not needed. You are a fabulous product of your environment, and despite what the world thinks of your relationship status, your crown cannot be removed by anyone else's hands but yours.

Though sadly, this is something many of us have done in one form or another. How, you ask? Oh, beautiful, in the simplest ways:

BY BELIEVING THE LIE

There is something to be said about all of the stuff society throws at us for being single. But the biggest downfall of it all is that some of us believe it. I have friends who are stunning, fabulous women of God and others who are the same minus their beliefs. Yet, no matter how amazing they are, it only takes one Facebook article about singleness to dump them into despair. Some would quickly say that it's due to low self-esteem, but because I know these ladies personally, I know it's much deeper. It's really because they've bought the lie. Society has brainwashed them into believing that their chances of happiness decrease with every tick-and-tock of the clock. They are under the impression that if they've reached a certain age, (and especially if they already have kids) that no "good man" will want them. Even worse, they feel that if they aren't supermodel thin, proportionally and perfectly voluptuous, or glamorous at all times of the day — that half of the male population wouldn't even bother to look their way.

Now, I'm sure many of you are judging my friends for everything I just listed, but before you throw stones, think about all of the lies you've bought into yourself. Such as - you're suddenly deemed unattractive since you haven't been on date in two months. Or do you think you're single because somehow botox equals beauty and society is telling you that you're aging poorly thanks to that forehead wrinkle? Beauty isn't the issue? Fine. What about when the world tells you that you're "too independent" and that's intimidating to a man? Is it your fault that success flows freely from you finger tips? Not at all — but the masses would have you believe it's the very reason why you're single. Did I strike a nerve? Good. Feel that irritation. Give a voice to that annoyance and call out the lies you've believed.

There you go. That's my girl, let's be real about this! We all have been there and if you just realized you're apart of the "society has me fooled" club, don't cower in shame. That revelation was the first thing needed for us to move forward. So, pat yourself on the back; you just had a breakthrough. Now that we're on the same page, let me debunk those lies.

I know a woman who is well into her 50s (though she looks much younger), who is a divorcee, with three kids (two adults and one teenager). Based on society and statistics, she should have just tried to stay with her husband because it's very unlikely that she'll ever marry again. I'm sure she may have even believed that at one point, but then something amazing happened.

She put her crown back on.

Men began to approach her at church, work and even online. But she was very particular about who she would give the time of day. Ultimately, she found herself on a dating site because she wasn't feeling the options popping up around her. One day, a man who was living hours away, sent her a message. But there was something special about this one. They conversed online, moved to talking on the phone and eventually began to date. And would you know that this couple just celebrated their 5-year anniversary? Now, had she continued to believe what "they say," she would have never opened herself up to the possibilities of what awaited her. Which prompts me to question, how many of us are missing our true blessings because we refuse to let go of the lies we believe?

Holding on to those 'stories' and stats is exactly what they want you to do. Yet, we know that God is able. Therefore, instead of limiting His abilities by putting Him in society's box, take off the lid! Let Him work and watch Him move! That's how you put your crown back on, Queen. But first, you have to stop believing the lie.

BY WATCHING THE CLOCK

A few years ago I was having dinner with a few people from I met at a church, all of whom were around 23 and a sprinkle of folks around my age (28). As we sat, the conversation followed it's typical path, flowing from talking about current church events, pop culture, music, so on and so forth until it made its way over to dating.

As usual, everyone shared their opinions on "the one" and what they thought their spouse could be like, what they wanted in a spouse, and a few even mentioned how they were thankful for their singleness until that time comes. Then one young lady blurted out: "Well, I'm 24, so he needs to hurry up!" Say what now? As one of the "elders" in the room, I looked over at her with an emotionless face and she looked back at all of us with an unapologetic one. All I could think was "Lord, if your plan is for her to wait until she's my age, please give her the grace to deal with that." I seriously wanted to ask her, "What clock are you watching?!" I mean, I get it, none of us are trying to be 98 strolling down the aisle. But who said it had to happen in your early twenties or that it can't happen in your late forties? You can give them my phone number because I'd love to hear their reasoning. Then I'd gladly explain to them why the God we serve is the Father of time. By mentally running against an imaginary clock, we often find ourselves taking whatever we can dig our claws into — thanks to the distress of thinking that it'll someday run out.

Though, when you know and believe that God is the author and finisher of your faith, you don't watch society's clock for your life, in any aspect. That's one of the lies we embed in our hearts and concern ourselves within our subconsciousness. Though, when you take a step back and "seek ye first the kingdom of heaven and all its righteousness," your mind is too preoccupied with things above to worry about what's out of your control. By taking time to align with God and His will for your life, you'll find yourself more concerned with fulfilling your purpose than you are with beating the clock. Put your crown back on and fix your eyes on God, Queen. He's working it out for you; you just have to let Him.

BY REMOVING YOUR CROWN

Imagine it: you're standing in a room full of attractive people, all chattering away about their lives and accomplishments. You're in the corner surveying the room without them even noticing. "Why am I the only one in here not chatting, right now?"

You're out with your friend and what seems like a never-ending cycle of men are approaching her. It's like you don't even exist. And by guy number five, you find yourself cutting your friend with eyes filled with envy, wishing you could get at least one dude to notice you.

You're in the fitting room, and everything is hugging on to that back-fat a little too tight. I mean, ever since you had the baby and Jon left, you've just put on so much weight! You feel less than and all you want to do is run home and watch TV, to fantasize about being as petite and curvy as the girls on the screen.

See Queen, we never consciously remove our crowns down, yet when we lower our heads in sorrow or thanks to low self-esteem, it simply slides off. And not for one-second should you think you're alone in these moments. We've all have had them, but the way I combat my emotional days is by remembering that God didn't make a single mistake when He made me, and He didn't make any with you either.

You are all beautiful, my love. There is no spot in you. (Song of Solomon 4:7 WEB)

Now, don't get me wrong, I know it's not always easy to believe this because you may not have a coke bottle shape, exotic features, or luscious locks of hair working in your favor — but you are "fearfully and wonderfully made" beyond your understanding. And the next time you begin to think about how Jon didn't stay or those guys didn't approach you, remember that God Himself called you priceless before you even existed. So to all of the people offering an opinion about who you are, remind them that God never asked them for one before and doesn't need it now. Close your ears to the negativity and go lay all of those concerns and cares at your Father's feet. He knows who you are, flaws and all. Even with His ability to see down to your every sin, He still loves you like crazy. And that's enough to make any Queen smile. Now, go put on that crown.

CHAPTER 2

Get Uncomfortable

WHAT'S HIS NAME? YOU know, your dating 'comfort zone.' Mine was James. We began dating during my senior year of high school and dated until my junior year of college. He was tall, dark, handsome, humble, had a smile that could light up any room and best of all, he was saved! He was a hardworking man even in high-school and never really stressed over anything. I know you're wondering why in the world aren't he and I married. Over a decade later, we both still get that question, haha!

Though, the truth is, as amazing as James sounds on paper he too had his flaws, like all of us. The biggest of them, for me, was that he was content with life in ways that I wasn't. When I was younger, it hardly phased me, but as I matured and started becoming the ambitious woman who would one day write this book, it became a deal-breaker. Sometimes from his eyes, my vision was just too big for him to fathom. Which was okay and still is for anyone who is like "James," but that wasn't for me. All of this paired with poor communication in a long-distance relationship led to James and I finally calling it quits.

When we officially ended our relationship, I was 22 - and in the years following I found myself going back to James and James coming back to me, more times than I could count. We were each other's comfort zones.

> **Comfort zone (/kemfert·zōn/):** a person where one feels they are safe to rest, in-between relationships — without actually ever committing to that particular situation-ship.

So I ask you again, who is your comfort zone? He has a name. He may be an ex, who you felt had the potential to be the one. He's a friend, who had the makings of a boyfriend but you guys never crossed that line or made it official. He's the one guy, who you text when you and your new dude split up, the one who's always down to be the buddy. Yep, that guy that just came to mind. Say his name aloud, because he is your comfort zone.

But you know, as cozy as his arms may feel, your comfort zone is the one place where growth can never occur. Love, it's time to get uncomfortable.

Running to his arms when you feel lonely, need a hug, need companionship or just need a little testosterone in your life is not healthy for you or them. And as much as men love to play as if they don't have emotional attachments to us, they do; it just manifests differently. But regardless of what he feels and says, you control you, and it's time for you to stop. It's a hard pill to swallow, especially when that's your relationship safe haven, but it's a lesson we all have to learn. I'm only a few months out of my "James comfort zone," and I will be honest, it was difficult to end that chapter. Not because I'm so helplessly in love with him or because I eagerly want it to work out for us, but if I'm honest: it's because that means I'm officially, fully, without a subtitle, single. And truly, as long as we had each other as a backup plan, neither of us weren't able to embrace that. I was dating with a safety net! Yes, I've dated and had boyfriends after he and I broke up, but I always had him in mind as a plan 'B' in case the other guy didn't last. In case that relationship didn't lead to the altar. In case I ended up wanting to have companionship. How selfish was I? Very. The conviction of "using" someone I cared so deeply about as a plan B was enough guilt to stop myself from letting it happen again. Though, the nail in the coffin to leave James alone in that capacity came from God.

I was sitting in my room one night, daydreaming about my "ideal" man. When I began to run the list over in my head again, it pretty much summed up James, with added characteristics, such as ambition. While that was never my intention, I quickly thought (in a joking manner), "Well, he's an option." And that's when I felt the conviction of my thought followed by the words that changed my entire view on dating:

"YOU KEEP A SAFETY NET BECAUSE YOU DON'T TRUST ME. YOU'RE WORRIED THAT MY PLAN WILL FAIL. BUT I'M GOD, I NEVER FAIL."

With my eyes full of tears and my heart full of guilt, I immediately began to repent. That was exactly what I was doing and as much as I prayed pretty prayers, claiming to be "waiting on God," I didn't want to actually have to wait on Him. I wanted Him to meet me wherever I was with the dude who was "going to be the one" because I made him the one. Claiming that he was Godsent, knowing good and well, he was just who I picked. And if that failed, well...I always had a plan B. Now, tell me, where in that cluster of chaos do you see me waiting on God? But if you were to tell me that, then I would have called you a hater and kept it moving like the Pharisee that I was.

Why am I telling you all of this? Other than the fact that it's aligned with this chapter, I don't want you to waste years like I did, claiming to be waiting on God when I wasn't. We can't fool Him with our trickery; He knows our hearts. Yet, He's such a gentleman. He will only convict us when we're ready. Like I said, I really did believe that I was doing it the right way. I had no doubt that I was actually waiting on God, but that day, at that moment, I realized the truth. The only person I was truly fooling, was myself. Take a moment to re-read that section and examine your heart and motives when it comes to romantic relationships. You may be amazed by how selfish and controlling you've actually been all of this time, claiming you were giving it to God. Then do something new — repent and sincerely give it to Him.

I know that dating a complete stranger is exhilarating and gives you the butterflies, but it's also one of the most frightening things you can do. It's not comfortable at all. But let me remind you, your comfort zone was a complete stranger at some point in time. Though, you managed to let him in enough to where after your precious heart is broken or disappointed, you run and allow him to hold it for just a second while till you get yourself together.

Don't do that anymore.

The next time a dating relationship ends or you feel like you need someone, get on your knees and pray. Open your Bible and read. Sit on a pillow and meditate — anything that will align you with God in your time of despair. The Bible says He's close to the brokenhearted [Psalm 34:18], so instead of taking your fragile pieces to a man, take them to God. Lay them at His feet and ask Him to mend you. Ask Him to fill you up in a way that leaves you better than you were before any of this began. Ask Him to fill you up so that you don't need a man to validate your worth. Rest in His care knowing that your love life is in the best possible care.

It's time to get uncomfortable so that God can bring you comfort.

CHAPTER 3

Never Settle!

A S I SIT HERE and type this book, I'm truly one of you. A single lady, waiting for love and leaning on God. So, as you read each word, imagine that I am writing this for you as much as I am writing it for myself. Like I said, I've settled before too, and it taught me never to settle again. Why? Well, as you can see, I am a Christian and I adore my relationship with God. Still, due to my yearning for a relationship (or so I thought), I found myself dating an agnostic.

> **Ag·nos·tic (/ag'nästik/):** a person who believes that nothing is known or can be known of the existence or nature of God or of anything beyond material phenomena; a person who claims neither faith nor disbelief in God. (Thanks, Google!)

"Ces, how in the world did that happen?!"

Easily — I thought I was ready for a relationship, to the extent that I was willing to date the guy who always liked me, to get it. He'd been pursuing me for some time after we went on a semi-blind date, set up by a mutual friend. We'd seen each other around, he always seemed to get nervous around me, and I always avoided him like the plague. Finally, our friend persuaded me to give him a chance because she just knew we were meant to be (yeah, I'm still single right? Right). I was in a bit of a super dry spell, hence the thirst, and so I agreed to the date. Needless to say, I came to my senses real quick and called her on the way home and told her "never again!"

"Wait, you said you dated him…as in more than just one date. What're you leaving out?"

That's the truth, we went on one date and it was awful…initially. Over the next few months, I noticed that he was becoming more and more confident around me and would make it a point to hold at least 5-10 minute conversation with me, every time we ended up in the same room. Being that we were a part of a tight circle, I ended up in this situation more often than not and slowly but surely, began to enjoy his company. Mind you, this entire time, I am fully aware of the fact that this man really isn't for me. We were so different that we were nearly polar opposites, with our religious views being our largest divide. But it came to a point where I didn't care.

One night, we decided to go out once more, and this time, I gave the man a fighting chance. Walls down, smile on, and more determination to enjoy this date than he ever imagined. Naturally, my positive vibes took hold of him, and he made sure I knew it. We laughed, we ate and laughed so much more. Yes, I thoroughly enjoyed myself! Even now, it's really one of the best dates I've ever been on.

Within weeks, we were seeing each other regularly and having dinner together every night. This lasted for several months until one day; I took the chance to see if I could be the one to bring him to Christ. Before eating anything, I always give thanks to God for my food. The entire time we dated, I would essentially do this alone, and he waited for me to finish, like the gentleman that he was. But I needed and still need, a Godly man. So, one day, while we were preparing to eat dinner, I looked over at him and asked if he could say grace. With the most sincere look on his face, he looked me in the eyes and said: "You know that's not my thing. But I'll wait for you, baby." I proceeded to pray alone, as usual. Then one day, I invited him to church, asking if he would give it a shot, at least for me. "Baby, organized religion isn't for me. No religion is for me, really. I don't believe in God anymore and even walking into your church would insinuate otherwise. I don't ask you to bend on this for me, please don't ask me to bend on this for you." You would think that was the nail in the coffin, but I'd be lying to you if I said it was. Yes, I was still seeing him after that. Confused, hurt and feeling more distant from God than ever, but I had a man. One with a heart of stone towards God, but I had one nonetheless. No judging allowed, just keep reading.

While driving back from an amazing date, I caught him staring at me when we were at a red light. I looked over, we locked eyes, and we both smiled. He reached over and ran his hands through my hair with a look I'd never seen before. He was so happy. At that moment, I think he'd fallen in love.

"What's on your mind, sir?" I asked.

He stared at me for a second before saying, "Baby, I can see us building an amazing life together. I've actually seen it since the first time I laid eyes on you. My friend, my wife, the mother of my kids... I've imagined you as it all before we had our first date."

With tears in my eyes, I was left speechless for a solid minute. When we pulled into my complex, he leaned over and gave me the sweetest kiss. When he leaned back, he stared at me and asked me to share what I was thinking. Smiling, I nervously let out the truth, "You know I want to raise my kids to love Christ as much as I do, if not much more. Would you be willing to do that with me? For the sake of "our" kids."

That was not what he wanted to hear. Within seconds, his mood shifted and he was deep in thought, searching for a reply that wouldn't ruin our night but would still give me a truthful and firm stance. "I would support you in anything that you want to do for our kids, but I wouldn't profess those beliefs in front of them. I'd want them to know how I felt. I wouldn't go to church with you, but I would make sure they did," he finally stated — and I finally got it.

The man that I'd been praying for; the man who would lead me closer to God instead of away. The man who would be the leader, preacher, teacher that God called him to be. The man who would be able to pray for me when I'm spiritually too weak to pray for myself. That man wasn't sitting across from me and that is the kind of man he would never want to be. We would never work, that much I could finally see.

I had settled. And not just for anyone, but with someone who wanted nothing to do with the God that I owe everything. I, me, myself, created the ultimate wedge between God and I, by choosing a man over us. Yes, he was great. Yes, he was a gentleman, and yes, he treated me like a princess. But he wasn't from God. He wasn't the one. But that's what happens when you settle, when you throw out your standards, and or lean on your own understanding.

No, settling doesn't mean that you end up with a guy who is awful and beats you or a guy who is a man who secretly rocks horns. That's the trick of the enemy that makes you think those things. The wrong guy isn't coming with a pitchfork and an upside down cross tattooed on his neck. He's coming in a package of everything that you dreamed of, while drenched in everything that you don't need. Now, don't get me wrong, I don't think he was a bad guy, but he certainly wasn't who God had in mind for me. Don't get me wrong, he wasn't a bad guy, but he certainly wasn't who God had for me — though, I learned so much from that short relationship. The greatest lesson being: never settle.

See, there comes a moment in this single journey when we hit that "something is better than nothing" period. Don't look away or roll your eyes, I'm not judging you. As you can see, I've been there too. It wasn't that we were desperate, but admit it, we were some-kind-of thirsty! Reason being, we reached a place in our singleness where we felt like having a man who wasn't too bad, who wasn't too far from our desires, who wasn't quite the person that God has for us, was okay. I mean, let society tell it, we should really get what we can get, while we can get it. After all, our chances to marry decrease every year, right? And when you've been single for what, 2+ years, you should really consider giving Donald-hit-on-and-date-every-girl from church a shot, you know? Nope. Unless God tells you to give Donald a shot, run in the opposite direction. Until God says you'll never marry, stop looking at your clock, wondering when it'll happen for you.

Instead of rushing to settle just to have *someone*, take your time and wait for *The One*. The One who will love you in ways you never thought possible. The One who will lead you closer to God and who'll guide your household as God called him to. The One who was born with the ability to love you like Christ loves the Church. The One who has dreamt of loving you before your first date could even start. The One who already has your name signed on the dotted line of his heart. He's going to love you well after your vixen shape has faded. He'll love you when you find it hard to love yourself, and he's even going to love you when you're wrinkly old and grey. That kind of love is worth waiting for, and that kind of love isn't what you receive when you settle. On the contrary, it's what you get when you wait.

Now, do me a favor, don't allow anyone or anything to coerce you into a situation that's not for you. Society, your family and maybe even some of the folks that you call friends, are eager to see you settle down with someone, and soon. But I'm a strong believer that if you rush down the aisle, you may find yourself rushing to divorce court. Take your time and enjoy your singleness — date, travel, live and get to know what traits you honestly desire and the ones you don't. If dating isn't your thing, make an effort to use that time to get to know yourself and get closer to God. Really, those should be two of your goals regardless of whether you like to date or not.

Getting closer to God not only draws you in line with His will, but it also keeps you out of His way, while teaching you to love yourself. Taking time to find out who you are, creates this undeniable rise of self-esteem that will constantly remind you why settling isn't an option and teaches you what unconditional love looks like from the inside out — which prepares you to give unconditional love, as well. As a matter of fact, if you're dating, I dare you to take a break and work on those two goals, you will be amazed at the difference it will make. When it's all said and done, settling will become a thing of the past because you'll finally be in a position to fully embrace who you truly are. And the *right one* won't be able to resist that.

CHAPTER 4

Waiting for Boaz

MANY CHRISTIAN WOMEN ARE either hot or cold when it comes to the dating scene. On one end of the pendulum, they're going on every date that comes their way, and on the other end, they're proudly proclaiming that they're "waiting on my Boaz!"

When I began my single and celibacy journeys (no, they didn't happen at the same time), I eventually found myself at the end of both extremes. One month, I'm on the dating scene, being treated to the city's finest, and within 30 days, I was shouting "ugh, forget it, Lord! I'm just waiting for Boaz." For those who haven't lived in both phases, I know you're probably wondering how I actually experienced them. Well, it was because I was so *wedding-ly* minded that I was nowhere near being good as a single. Every guy that showed interest had my undivided attention. Every gesture was examined under a "could this be the one" microscope. I was driving myself into desperation, investing emotionally in men who didn't deserve it and wasted more time than necessary by trying to *help* God bring my Ruth-like-Boaz to fruition. Yet, the worst part was I truly began to feel insecure about being single. I became so uncomfortable alone. To the extent that I derailed from my old-fashioned dating approach and began being the aggressor. Yes, ma'am. I began to be the 'man' and basically worked to pursue him. For instance, if he wasn't calling or texting me enough, I started to call and text enough for the both of us. The need to feel wanted, the desire to feel needed, thinking I was only as good as my relationship status; it all became a problem. After being frustrated with how long God seemed to be taking, it all finally clicked. God wasn't moving for me because I no longer depended on Him.

And even after that revelation, it all didn't really hit home until one night when I was out. There were about 4 of us, sitting in the middle of a lounge. Looking, feeling, smelling, and acting like a million bucks dripped from our fingertips. We were definitely the definition of the saying "birds of a feather flock together" because as fly we were, we were also the thirstiest lil' cluster that you ever did see. Looking fierce on the scene, yet we all came with a common goal: to meet a guy. All dolled up hoping that we'd catch the eye of the right one. Sitting there prim and proper, but reeking of thirst and desperation. We rolled together like close girlfriends, but the only thing that really bonded us was our love for God and our longing to be in a relationship. We were all discontent in our singleness and refusing to fully trust God. We were all hoping for Boaz to turn the corner, any corner, and sweep us off our feet.

Yes, the thirst was real, and I finally saw it.

As I looked around at the gorgeous group, tears began to take over my eyes because it was then that I looked into three mirrors. Hurt. Desperation. Wanting to settle down. Thinking we needed a man. Broken. We were all broken...I was broken. That night, I went home and literally laid prostrate on my floor and cried out to God — begging Him for forgiveness, asking for His peace, demanding the removal of the desperation, and admitting that only He could quench my thirst. And that night is when I realized, that even though I was "trusting God" for Boaz, I displayed not a single characteristic of Ruth.

When Boaz and Ruth met, two very simple things were occurring:
1. Ruth was working to pursue her purpose.
2. Boaz only took notice of Ruth because she was working.

Let's break this thing down:

RUTH WAS WORKING WHEN SHE MET BOAZ.

> *¹Naomi had a relative of her husband's, a mighty man of wealth, of the family of Elimelech, and his name was Boaz. ²Ruth the Moabitess said to Naomi, "Let me now go to the field, and glean among the ears of grain after him in whose sight I find favor." She said to her, "Go, my daughter." ³She went, and came and gleaned in the field after the reapers; and she happened to come to the portion of the field belonging to Boaz, who was of the family of Elimelech. (Ruth 2:1-3 WEB)*

Ruth was in the field and truly minding her own business when she caught Boaz's eye. She wasn't out flaunting her singleness, wallowing with her girlfriends about how much she needed a man, or wearing her sexiest outfit to bait one. She was in her purpose and truly unconcerned with anything else. A stranger in a foreign land, her only goal was to help Naomi and take care of the woman she loved like a mother. The Bible makes it clear that Ruth took her time in making sure that she collected enough grain for them to have leftovers. Yes, she was essentially the Proverbs 31 woman, minus the husband and kids, yet just as selfless in the pursuit to take care of home.

Now, let's pause right here and be honest with each other, for one-second. If you're waiting on your 'Boaz,' that also means that you need to be 'Ruth' to some extent first, right? Yet, so many women are literally sitting in the house, refusing to move in purpose until their husband arrives — as if Boaz is going to come knocking on the door and sweep them off their feet. Don't get me wrong, nothing is impossible with God, but the Bible clearly tells us that 'faith without *works* is dead.'

You need to move, live, experience life, and pursue your purpose! In passionately going after what God called you to do, you're not only showing God that you trust Him, but you're also saying you can submit to His will for your life. See, in this phase of things, Ruth's actions not only show that she's concerned with the things of God, but it also reveals that she willingly submitted to them as well. Take a second and look in a mirror. Do you think God would send 'Boaz' to a woman who isn't willing to submit to Him but is begging for a man? If He did, not only would He be giving you a relationship that you're not ready for, but He'd also essentially hand-deliver His replacement. Yes, my love, you would make this man an idol in your life. You would worship him like he is your god.

I know that stung a bit; it hurt like hell when I realized it too.

And no, this isn't me judging you or assuming I know your story. But it's your sister-in-Christ being honest and transparent with you, in a way that others may not. God is a jealous God, and He is not going to bring you someone to take His place — though, the minute the enemy sees the insecurity, he most certainly will. That's why you have to become content in every season of your life, especially this one. God forbid you get so bogged down with trying to get into a relationship that you never learn to enjoy being single. And God forbid you fall for the bait and start a life with someone He never intended for you be with, in the first place.

Ruth was at peace with her widow status, and I truly believed that if God never allowed Boaz to see her, she would have been just fine living out her days with Naomi.

Are you there yet?

If God didn't plan for you to get married, would you still say He is good? If He called you to a life of singleness, would you still serve Him? I know you're giving those questions the glare of death, but these are things you actually have to consider. We all do because despite what we desire, we don't know what the end is going to be. But say this is your fate, are you really willing to put these years on hold, hoping it's not? If you said 'no,' good! If you said 'yes,' girl... stop. You are too smart, too beautiful, too worthy, and too wonderfully made to spend your best years waiting for the rest of your years. Get out and live!

Never be afraid to take yourself on a date. Travel with your girlfriends or alone. See the world, gain experience, and live a life so full that no matter what God has in store, you can say, "I was present for my days. I was here!" It's not always ideal to think this way, but when you are bold enough to treat yourself to the things and places you wish to share with a mate, you'll find that it's a lot easier to say 'no' to the counterfeits who're trying to waste your time and take up space. Go live, my love. Go. Live!

BOAZ ONLY TOOK NOTICE OF RUTH BECAUSE SHE WAS WORKING.

[5]Then Boaz said, "On the day you buy the field from the hand of Naomi, you must buy it also from Ruth the Moabitess, the wife of the dead, to raise up the name of the dead on his inheritance." [6]The near kinsman said, "I can't redeem it for myself, lest I endanger my own inheritance. Take my right of redemption for yourself; for I can't redeem it." [7]Now this was the custom in former time in Israel concerning redeeming and concerning exchanging, to confirm all things: a man took off his shoe, and gave it to his neighbor; and this was the way of legalizing transactions in Israel. [8]So the near kinsman said to Boaz, "Buy it for yourself," then he took off his shoe. [9]Boaz said to the elders, and to all the people, "You are witnesses today, that

I have bought all that was Elimelech's, and all that was Chilion's and Mahlon's, from the hand of Naomi. ¹⁰Moreover Ruth the Moabitess, the wife of Mahlon, I have purchased to be my wife, to raise up the name of the dead on his inheritance, that the name of the dead may not be cut off from among his brothers, and from the gate of his place. You are witnesses today." ¹¹All the people who were in the gate, and the elders, said, "We are witnesses. May Yahweh make the woman who has come into your house like Rachel and like Leah, which both built the house of Israel; and treat you worthily in Ephrathah, and be famous in Bethlehem. (Ruth 4:5-11 WEB)

Had Ruth decided to go back to her parents, and not work in the fields to take care of Naomi, or to do any of the countless other things that she could have picked from; she would have never been in the position to meet Boaz. In fact, she would have been completely outside of God's will. Isn't it interesting how one decision that seems so small and insignificant, catapulted Ruth to a new place in life? Not only did this man find her worthy to be his wife [Ruth 4:5-11], but even before that phase, he saw fit to take care of her. He also made sure she didn't have to strain herself to work for food, telling the men to be gentle with her, and seeing to it that the women dropped more grain for her to have and that she didn't *thirst*. Boaz was a man of valor and respected this woman of purpose to the utmost.

If that isn't worth waiting for, I don't know what is.

Evidently, Ruth did not do something many of us are guilty of doing: she didn't take Boaz's kindness for granted. She didn't take the favor that God was bestowing on her through him lightly. She showed gratitude for not only what he was willing to do, but also for him showing her respect for who she was. He knew her story, which also means he knew she was a widow. He knew that she hardly had the means to support herself, let alone Naomi. Yet, he didn't see this as a sign of weakness or something to look down on her for. He saw her strength and her determination. As I mentioned earlier, Ruth was about her business and Boaz admired that about her.

What about you?

Are you in pursuit of your purpose? Are you so busy being about your Father's business, that 'Boaz' has to spot you while you're on the move? Are you working with so much diligence that the man of your dreams would admire your tenacity? Do these questions have you reevaluating your life? I hope so!

See, as a woman, you're called to be a man's help-meet; not his footstool, extra child, or his lazy fly wife. I wholeheartedly believe that each of us has a purpose to complete in our singleness and others to manifest in our relationship (dating and marriage). But if all you want to do is sit around doing nothing before 'Boaz' arrives and after you've met him, then plan to do all of that alone. Boaz is an Ephesians 5 man, longing for a Proverbs 31 woman. And the last time I checked, she wasn't sitting around worrying about what time the club was jumping or which sugar-daddy she could trap. She moves with intention and is unapologetic about her desire to fulfill God's will. Maya Angelou said it best, "a woman's heart should be so lost in God that a man has to seek Him to find her." Get focused on Him and let it all play out as only He could plan, because it truly only takes God giving you an ounce of direction or a sprinkle of favor to change your entire life from good to great, and your relationship status from single to happily taken. But it only happens this way if you're in His will and trust His way.

So, for those of us waiting on our Boaz, be mindful of what it takes to first be more like Ruth.

CHAPTER 5

Side Chicks Never Prosper

'M WALKING OUT OF one of my favorite stores, and as I started my car, a new BMW comes flying into the spot next to me. This dark-skinned cutie jumps out like he's in a rush, so instead of pulling off and making him wait, I motion for him to walk by. But then he does something I didn't expect; he asks me to roll down my window. A little confused and always cautious, I crack my window just enough to hear him. "Sorry, I wasn't rushing to go in there...I was rushing to stop you." Ahh, shucks now. "I saw you walking across the street and I'm about to be late running back to work, but I couldn't miss the chance to meet you. My name is Derek. May I have yours?"

Well, isn't he assertive?

Picture it: he wasn't too tall (but I'm pretty short, so that's okay), dark-skinned, handsome, great smile, clearly a regular at the gym, and from the looks of it, he was doing well financially. And even with all of that, for some reason, before I really even gave it any thought, I blurted out: "Tasha, my name is Tasha." We shared a few genuine laughs, exchanged numbers, and then we went our separate ways.

Over the next few days, we would have nonchalant *textversations*, and I kept wanting to tell him my real name, but it never seemed like the right time. Then, before I knew it, the red flags started to hit the field:

Derek: Hey! How's your day going?

Me: Going good! Yours?

D: Same. What do you have planned for the weekend?

Me: Nothing much, it's my only free weekend this month, so I'm taking it easy.

D: I understand — I'm actually heading to Texas to see my family tomorrow.

D: But I want to link up with you soon.

D: Send me a full body pic.

D: What kind of stuff do you like to do?

Pause. Did you peep that?

Now, I know some may not see anything wrong with this, but let me tell you why it's a problem for me. For one, we'd just met. The fact that he's asking for a full body picture shows that he's more interested in how I look than how I think.

Secondly, he's testing me. Asking for a full body picture is a sure-fire way for him to see what kind of woman he's dealing with. Would I send a picture from a day at the beach? The club? Church? Maybe a nude? The dating scene is saturated with women who feel that they're in desperate need of a man, to the point that if sending a half-naked or naked picture of themselves guarantees a date and call back, they'll do it.

Lastly, call me old-fashioned, but the only reason he wants to see my body is to see if I'm smashable.

Smashable (/smaSH-ah-ble/): attractive or at least acceptable enough, to want to engage in sexual relations with. (Ces-ism)

If I were to send a picture and pass "the test," he would be completely ready to move forward. He would then think I'm worthy of taking out and know exactly how to handle me; all based on how I responded to that simple ask. So, I didn't.

I ignored that request and replied to the rest, and to my surprise, we continued speaking. Though, as the days went on, it became very clear that something was up with this guy and I didn't like it. But as the Lord says, "what is done in the dark will come to light" and oh, did it come!

D: *Hey! How's your day going?*

Me: *Hey! Good and yours?*

D: *Mine is going great! Up packing for Texas now. You?*

Me: *Just settled in from my run.*

D: *Cool, cool. So, I was wondering, do you have a dude that you're seeing? Like someone that you're just talking to? Dating? Or living with? If so, I'm okay with that.*

Me: *Would you really be okay with that?*

D: *Haha, I'll take that as a 'no.'*

Me: *Well, I'm just asking…would you really be okay with that?*

D: *Yeah, I would.*

Me: *"Do you have a woman 'that you're seeing?*
Like someone that you're just talking to? Dating? Or living with?'"

D: *I see what you did there. Lol! Would you be okay with that?*

Me: *Well, I would want to know.*

D: *Haha, well let's just say. I have my situation here and you have yours there. And we can have this too…so we're good to keep this thang moving.*

Thinking: What in the?! No, we won't!!

Me: *Actually, I don't have a situation over here. I'm single. If I had a man, I would've neeeevverrrrr given you my phone number.*

D: *Oh, really?*

Me: *Really. So, you and your girl take care. I hope things work out for you two, and I pray you become faithful to her sooner than later. God bless!*

D: Oh, it's like that?!

D: I was just playing, I don't have a girl.

Me: Suuurrrrrrrrrrrree, haha!

D: So we're done? You're just giving up on us?

Me: We never started anything for me to give up. Take care of your girl, sir!

D: Oh, come on. Anyway, how old are you?

I never responded, and we never spoke again.

As annoyed as I was with him, I couldn't help but wonder how he got the nerve to even think it was okay to approach me with this in the first place! He literally asked me to be a side-chick as if I would leap at the chance. That's when I realized; he was bold enough to ask me because someone was once weak enough to accept. A beautiful woman who had low self-esteem, unable to see her worth, and the thought that she was only good enough to be something on the side, said "yes." That gorgeous woman opted to be his appetizer, instead of her waiting for a man who would appreciate her as a main course. That breaks my heart.

Have you ever been the side chick?

And before you turn up your nose at me, know that I'm not judging or trying to insult you, because guess what? I have been one.

Oh stop, don't play shocked. I'm not perfect.

And even though I was only 17, the lessons that I learned through that experience stayed with me for a lifetime. It wasn't worth it then and I'm wiser because of it now. But I hope you are too because just as many of us have settled to be the side chick, we've also been the woman who's unbeknownst to us, was being cheated on. It didn't feel good, and actually, it hurt like hell. You feel like your insides are burning and you are disgusted by the fact that he would even touch another woman when he was the only person allowed to touch you. The betrayal, the heartache, and the pain; it all feels absolutely unbearable at first. I remember crying, sobbing, being unapologetically distraught; but it was only the manifestation of what I put into the atmosphere. The heartbreak I was reaping, was simply the harvest of what I had sown.

SO, WHAT SEEDS ARE YOU PLANTING?

You know the guy you're talking to who has a girl, but it's clearly not working out with her? Or the guy who just wants to be friends with you, but he's not willing to commit to you or leave her? How about the man you've been dating and having sex with while he's constantly telling you he's going to leave his girlfriend or wife; but now just isn't "the right time." Yes, every text or sext, intimate conversation, lustful thought, sensual kiss, or sexual escapade is a seed, my love. And just as you are sowing, remember one day, you will reap. The worst part is that you can't control when the harvest will sprout, and you can't determine how long it will stick around, all you know is that it. is. coming.

ARE YOU EXPECTING A HARVEST?

Though, I seriously hope you aren't. I pray for you if you are, because long after he is gone, she is healed, and all of your lives have moved on, you may begin to see the seeds start to sprout. We know that God is fair and He'll never put more on us than we can bear, but keep in mind, He is also just. So, if you're around here sowing sin, you should also expect to see the consequences eventually. I know, that's an ugly truth that no one wants to hear, but I'd rather share the truth with you in love, than for you to be caught off guard and ball your eyes out with pure disdain towards yourself or God.

BUT THE DAMAGE CAN MINIMIZED.

Step back and look at what you're doing or have done, and truly begin to repent for being so selfish. Yes, you, I, we were selfish in the midst of it all. We didn't care about the woman on the other side of it all, the kids (if applicable) who were impacted by the strain between their parents, and most importantly, how much we really hurt God — yeah, God. Imagine creating someone and knowing everything about them, down to the number of hairs on their head. You have this beautiful life planned for them and (possibly) a spouse, that will love them like no other. Now, realistically, God didn't intend for this person's life to be perfect or easy, but it was always intended for them to be blessed no matter the circumstances. And despite the bumps in the road that He knew would be there, He never wanted any of us to get involved with adultery.

"But what about him? I'm not cheating alone!"

Regardless of how that man has behaved and no matter what his relationship is like with his spouse, God is holding everyone accountable for their own (individual) actions. So yes, the man involved will see his own consequences come to fruition, but come Judgment Day, you can only attest for yours. Don't take that as a threat from me; it's just a reminder from God. The same God who truly loves you too much to let you fall for a man who means you no good. The very God who cares more about you than you do for yourself. Yes, THE GOD who gave His only Son for you and I. That God, that God right there, He is watching, and every time you or I created a soul-tie to someone who we weren't even supposed to connect with, or compromised our faith for anything; we broke His heart. Not just because we've sinned, but because He has to be fair and allow the consequences of our actions to eventually manifest.

We chose to sin with our free will and therefore, we (sometimes without knowing) also chose to reap the harvest from what we have sown. As frightening as that may be, it's the one thing that's non-negotiable. Even David, a man after God's own heart, saw consequences from his affair with Bathsheba through the death of their newborn son. Again, I would never wish you harm or for you to experience anything that tragic, yet we have to accept that we will always reap what we sow.

No good comes out of being the other woman because no one leaves that situation unscathed — in fact, it tends to always have innocent casualties instead. And from what I know and have experienced firsthand, we all have at least been the woman who was being cheated on. Don't inflict that pain on your sister-in-Christ just to have a piece of a man. If he really wanted to be with you, he would. If he seriously wanted to leave her, he would have. If he truly wanted you to be the only one, there would be no other option. He wants his stable relationship, and he wants his fun on the side, but understand that you deserve an entire man. Not one that you have to share, who has to leave you by a certain time, or who can't talk to you after a particular hour, or who can't introduce you to his family.

YOU ARE A PRIZE!

Whoever it is you're supposed to be with will adore you, not for how good you look on his arm or for how good you are in bed, but for how full you make his heart. He will make you his wife and not his side dish. He will wake up and thank God the minute he sees your face. He will treasure you like the priceless Proverbs 31 woman that you are and would never make you feel less than so that he can feel greater. And when you're living that life out, the last thing you would want is some chick popping up and butting in. So, don't be that woman now. Don't become her, ever again. You were created for something greater and with a divine purpose. Remember, God, deemed you priceless before you were born...besides, side chicks never prosper.

CHAPTER 6

Why You're Single

O KAY, WE'VE TOUCHED ON a few topics that may have rubbed you the wrong way, or made you uncomfortable, but above all, hopefully, they've made you take a closer look at yourself. But now that we've touched on all of those topics, I'm ready to get down to the nitty-gritty; it's time to talk about why you are single in the first place.

Let me guess — you are financially stable, you love the Lord, you are extremely independent, you are beautiful, dope, fly, and the definition of a bad chick, but for the life of you, you can't figure out why you're still single. All of your friends think it must be because you're picky; they can't fathom a world where dudes aren't banging down your door. Your colleagues are wondering when love will find its way to you because you just seem like the perfect catch. And your family is waiting for the day that the one finally finds you because they're tired of you coming to the family events solo or with that ride-or-die homegirl.

Do you know why I can describe you so well? Yep, I am you. We are one. Sisters-in-Christ looking like the same picture in a different frame. So, beyond knowing what people think and are saying to you and about you, I know how frustrated you are about being single too. Maybe not all of the time, but there are days when you wonder "when will it happen for me, Lord?"

BUT WHY ARE YOU SINGLE?

Early in my singleness, I remember getting so frustrated with the fact that I had to even ask. I mean I checked ever box: I was committed to waiting until marriage, attending church multiple times a week, volunteering, and genuinely supported those around me who were getting married. I was doing everything that I was *supposed* to do! That's when God said, "Ces, but it's not about *you*." And in that moment, it was finally obvious that all I had been focusing on was how I felt, wanted to feel, and when I would get into the relationship of my dreams. All of that "I" focus would have graduated to "we," which consists of me plus man, minus God. That relationship would have become an idol, and truthfully, that is probably why you aren't in one now too.

If you're constantly praying for your prince charming to come in on his white horse or waiting for a man to come and make your life better, you've already made an idol out of someone you haven't even met yet. This makes me think of the Israelites when they were asking for a king [1 Samuel 8-15]. God kept telling them they didn't need one, but they so desperately wanted to be like every other nation around them. They didn't care if the man was truly qualified, they just wanted to be able to say that like their neighbors, they too had a king. With ample warning, God made it happen, but before it even began, He warned them that their king would fail them — Saul eventually did.

Are you begging for a king like the Israelites while God is steady telling you, you don't need one? See, that man isn't going to make you feel adequate, neither will that relationship make you feel complete, nor will hearing someone call you 'baby' change your life. The Israelites didn't fail because Saul was made their king, they were a corrupt people before he even arrived; but the point God was trying to make for them (and you) is that a man won't solve those problems. That lack, longing, and desire can only be filled by God and you. He will supply that lack and He will make you whole, all of which you have to be before you get into an intimate relationship. If not, I hate to say it, but you will find yourself even more broken and lost than you were before you entered the relationship, because the minute that man doesn't meet your expectations or decides to move on to the next chick, you will be crushed — all because you were putting all of your hope into a man.

We all know that as good as we can be, we are still flawed creatures, which is why you need to be mature (mentally, emotionally and spiritually) before you decide to enter into a relationship. If not, that man will become your god, and you will do anything to keep him, even if it means losing you and neglecting God.

But like the Israelites, God doesn't desire for you to go through unnecessary pain. Though, at the same time, you are also open to having free will. So, if you so choose to get into a relationship, regardless of if it's the right time or not, you will, but just as we talked about side chicks reaping the consequences of their actions, your choices will leave you facing the same.

Is it really worth it?

Would you rather have any man instead of the right one for you? Would you prefer to date a person who will bring you more pain than joy, in the end, just to say you had someone for the time being? I'm not saying you can't date, but what I am saying is don't date men that you can't see a future with. Have standards and be true to them. Set boundaries and adhere to them. Trust God, and let Him lead. I have been single for several years at this point, and while my dating life is fine and fun, I refuse to become involved with someone who I know isn't for me. If I can sense that this man and I will not work, I don't drag it on for the free dinners and warm hugs — nope, bye! We can be cool and we can be cordial, but I'm not interested in being a space filler or having one. I deserve to be happy and with someone that is right for me, and so do you!

Now granted, this single life can get a little lonely, and I use that word lightly. But come on, it's okay to admit it — there are times when you are good on your own, happy to go on dates alone, fine to go out with just the girls, and cool with kicking it with the crew on the weekends. However, you also desire to have that intimacy that you can only get from a significant other. And when I say intimacy, I don't mean sexually, because true intimacy is far beyond that. It's a connection with someone which reaches beyond the physical, down to the depths of your souls, where you become tied together through truth, emotions, transparency, conflict, and the desire to make it work on all levels that the physical can't even begin to comprehend. That is true intimacy.

When was the last time you really experienced *that*? Better yet, is it what you want?

If you said yes, you've already begun to unfold the second reason why you're single. See, as a woman of virtue and a woman who knows her worth, you have given up the need to be with just any man and have decided to wait for the one that feels like 'the man.' And you're definitely not single due to lack of interest because you literally have dudes who're down to make this thing official, but you'd rather wait for Mr. Right.

But what does Mr. Right look like?

Once upon a time, I actually had a list detailing the man who would steal my heart and change my last name. He was tall, dark, handsome, fit, focused, financially stable, cultured, a dreamer and a doer. And he'll probably still be all of those things, but that list no longer exists. And if you have one, figuratively or literally, I would like for you to throw it away...like now.

No ma'am, don't give me that face, haha!

I'm not telling you something that'll hurt you, but I'm disclosing to you something that you need to hear. That list will be the reason why no man ever measures up. Not because he isn't real, but because you're looking for everything on it, leaving no room for compromise and for God to be God. You're essentially telling Him, 'You don't really have it all worked out, so let me help You!' Allow me to let you into a little secret; I've talked to my married friends and asked them what happened to their lists (because they all had one), and they admitted that their husbands and wives didn't add up to what they'd imagined, but surpassed it. One of my friends literally said, "I couldn't have built the man that God blessed me with, even if I tried." So, no, I'm not asking you to throw away your standards, but to remove the instruction manual to the kind of love that can only be built by faith.

Faith that God knows what you need better than you do. Faith that God has plans for you, to prosper you and not to harm you, but to give you a hope and a future. Faith that God can see beyond what looks like the perfect a match in the present, to the type of man you'll need in the future. That kind of love, that everlasting-till-death-do-us-part kind of love, that you dream about.

Do you believe God can make it happen, even if you can't see it right now? If you're having a hard time seeing it, reach out to some of your married friends (saved or not, I've asked both) and ask about their lists. Ask if their spouse lives up to what they wanted and ask if they really had it all figured out when they made *that list*.

And before I let you go on to the next chapter, let me just explore one more possibility as to why you're still single: it's just not your time.

"Ces, I have been single for ten years and haven't had a solid prospect in six. Now, come on!!"

Girl, I hear you! I wouldn't dare sit here and minimize anyone's story because doing so, says that your journey is invalid and that is the last thing I'd ever believe. Though, I have to ask: would you rather marry three times just to say you *have* loved or marry once and say you *are* loved?

If you would rather spend the rest of your life with the right person, instead of going from one divorce hearing to the next, you will have to wait. And before you run off thinking of why you're waiting, take a moment and realize that your spouse is waiting too. He's the best man in weddings, throwing bachelor parties, and seeing his friends start families just like you are. He's tired of being a groomsman and not the groom. But like you, he's not interested in settling but wants to settle down.

"If that's the case, why aren't we together?"

God does everything in *His* perfect timing, and you all will meet when you're supposed to. I don't have the slightest clue as to when or where that'll happen. Maybe it will be after you fulfill a part of your purpose, or after the kinks are worked out of you both. Whatever the reason may be, trust that it's better to wait for God than it is to rush ahead of His plans. You deserve to be courted, desired, pursued, treated like a Queen and loved unconditionally — and all of these will come in time, but are you willing to wait?

Okay, I lied, there's one more theory to explore: what if God called you to be single?

Some of you looked at this page like I just called you out of your name. Trust me; I know this is the last thing that you want to hear or even think about. But what if this really is your fate? What if God really does prefer for you to be single for the rest of your life? Would you be okay with that? Would you debate and fight His will? Would you see this as a curse instead of a blessing?

"Ces, be real — how could that be a blessing?!"

Easily, because anything that God sends forth is a blessing to the one who He intends to receive it, that's how. If God has called you never to get married, or to never bear children; then so be it. But that doesn't mean you will have a less fulfilled life than the woman who does.

Your calling may very well, consist of a purpose that requires you to be selfless and fully committed to God, without obligation to anyone else. As a wife, you are committed to God, but you are also submissive to your husband and a caregiver to your children. There is very little room for you to operate in spontaneous assignments with a family in the picture. Not to say, the wife can't be used to do more than what meets the eye, but any wife and mother will tell you, she has to think of her family at all times.

Do you have a pet? Okay, think of how you can't just up and leave town without making arrangements to ensure that they are taken care of. And if you take them with you, you have to stop and let them use the restroom, see to it that they have plenty to eat and drink, make sure you stop to give them time to move and stretch, bring toys to keep them occupied, bring pee-pee pads in case you can't stop in time: responsibilities.

So, while God is blessing a couple with a marriage and kids, He's also able to bless a single person with flexibility and spontaneity to do His will. It's truly not a curse, and if that is what God has called you or me to, I pray that He gives us peace to appreciate it and skin thick enough to withstand what the world will say about it. His standards are not theirs, and theirs are nowhere near His; but I assure you, they will try to belittle the lives of those who are called to be single as if they fulfilled nothing because they were never married or parented a child. Even worse, the world will attempt to guilt that person into believing that they will live a life full of loneliness and hardship; reflecting pity for them every time they can. But the truth is, if that is someone's purpose and they chose to see it through with vigor, that person will fulfill more than the world could ever imagine — simply because that person will have lived a life pleasing to God.

CHAPTER 7

You're Thirsty. Yep, you!

I CAN ONLY IMAGINE the look you just made when you read this title of this chapter, haha! No, I don't know your life but I think I know a bit of your story — and you know I'm quick to tell you that you're not alone and in this instance, you're not.

Remember how I said I would eventually take over as the pursuer in the dating game? Calling enough for the both of us, texting more than needed, as classy as I am just being way too aggressive. But that was because I was thirsty. Thirst-tay. If that man showed me interest and we were close to being official, I figured I'd help expedite the process, but little did I know it was the very reason the process. Little did I know that was the very reason the process was delayed even more.

See, of all the real men that I know, none of them are fond of an aggressive woman. Though, the men who act more like boys enjoy being pursued and even do their part to make sure the chase doesn't stop. They say all of the right things, and give you just enough attention to appease you while doing the bare minimum to *keep you* wanting more. Yes, the thirst is a dangerous place for ladies of virtue, and it's the breeding ground for less than men. With that in mind, let's break this thing down because the thirst isn't always what it seems.

THIRST: THE PROBLEM. THE CURE.

We all have a desire to be wanted, and it's truly a natural feeling. Yet, the greatest impact of the "thirst" is that it changes how we express that yearning. We go from saying that we want an organic relationship to forcing one, but at what cost? Let's tally it up: underestimating your worth when you finally realize that he was never that into you, the amount of time you invest into someone who wasn't ready for you, and how much effort you pour into a bottomless situationship. It may not sound like much to some, but when you do this over and over again, you end up being drained, disgruntled, and depressed or even worse, desperate.

I'm not writing this from hearsay, I'm sharing this from experience.

There's a guy that I'd met a few years ago that we'll call Kendrick. We met through mutual friends, and Kendrick and I ended up talking ('talking': getting to know each other to potentially date; though it's nothing exclusive until then) for a bit. On paper, Kendrick and I were perfect. We both had a burning passion for Jesus, we were both doing well in our careers, and our parents even used a similar process to determine our names, haha! Listen, no one could tell me that he wasn't "the one," which made me anxious and led to me trying to expedite the process (it's okay, you can roll your eyes. I did too). I quickly became too aggressive for him, and while he was feeling me, I was also terrifying him. He wanted something real, but at the same time, it was becoming clear that due to my anxiousness, or maybe fate, he didn't want it with me. And thus, the situation ended.

Months go by, and we do this weird tango, where we keep in touch and ignore each other at the same time. While this was going on, I was doing the work. The work to get to know and love myself. Having sessions with a life coach, reading self-help books, attacking my issues that led to this behavior: truly doing the work. I was tired of being so parched over guys who couldn't quench my thirst. I needed freedom from that phase of my life and wanted to be ready for what was meant to last the rest of my lifetime. One day, I text him to see if he's going to a Christian event taking place that weekend, but of course, I start out with the nonchalant "Hey! How's it going?" He replies, "Okay. You?" Now, I was never his girlfriend and barely would consider myself a friend, but I knew him well enough to know that something is wrong. Without hesitation, my fingers composed the next text:

> *Me: Is everything okay, love? Do you need me to pray for you or about anything?*
> *Kendrick: No, everything isn't okay. My step-mom isn't doing well, and the doctors said that it's not looking good, at all.*
> *Me: Oh no, I'm so sorry to hear that! (and I proceeded to send him a long a genuine prayer, covering his entire family for whatever God intended to happen)*
> *Kendrick: Thank you so much, Ces! You have no idea how much I needed that!!*

We continue to text for a while, but that was clearly all that God wanted me to do, and I obeyed. The very next morning, I receive a call from a mutual friend thinking she was calling to talk about the death of Prince, but instead, she was uttering to me that Kendrick's step-mom, the person one that I'd just prayed for less than 24-hours ago, had passed away. As soon as I hung up with her, I received a text from Kendrick, confirming the news and thanking me for praying for him and his family. The next thing I know, we're on the phone and he's telling me about her last hours on earth and how she was at peace, which gave him solace. He invites me to the funeral and I attended the funeral to show my support (not sitting with the family of course) and spoke to him for maybe 3 minutes afterwards. That would be the last time that we speak until about a month later, when I get a random text from him asking if I was free to hang out that night. Now, even with my "no same day-dates[1]" rule, I said yes, and we ended up sitting in the house watching a cult classic together. The vibe was mellow and a little flirty, but we were both dedicated to our individual celibacy journey's, so nothing happened. Mmm hmm, get your mind out of the gutter. Haha!

While we were there, he ended up telling how he was getting ready for his first work trip since his step-mom passed and how he wasn't sure if he was ready for it. We, of course, talk about a plethora of things before and after that, but that moment of vulnerability stuck out to me. So, the next day, with that heavy on my heart, I run to the store to make a little gift bag for him; with the hope that it'll make this difficult trip a little more comfortable. It wasn't anything extravagant (to me), but ended up being a cute little "travel pack" since he was always on-the-go for work. Within the hour, I head over to his place to drop the gift off (I'm not creepy, he knew I was coming) and he was so appreciative when he saw it in my hand!

But something was off.

The carefree vibe that consumed the room the night before was long gone, and despite the fact that I was just sitting on the sofa, I literally felt like I was in the way. Not afraid of owning the moment, I say that I should go and he assured that I was fine and welcome to stay for a bit. But again, something was off. Within minutes, the vibe was so weird that I decided to head out and unlike any other time that we saw each other, he didn't walk me to my car or even seem warm when we said bye. The minute I got in the car, I said a quick prayer, started my car and drove off. And to this very day, as these words roll

---

[1] The 'no same day-dates' rule: If a guy hits me up and asks me on a date for that same day, I decline. My time is limited, valuable, and it's not fair for him to assume otherwise. Yes, I love spontaneity, but I also appreciate someone taking a moment to plan our time together, instead of feeling like the idea of a date was an after-thought.

from my mind into this chapter, I haven't heard from him. He never even reached out to say "thank you" for the gift. Oh man, do I feel the look on your face! Yes, ma'am. Not so much as a peep! Though, this is where the peace of the cure comes in; because had I done that on my own accord, I'd be pissed. I would feel used, neglected and tossed to the side like an old Christmas toy. Yet, I can truly say that that gift was only purchased because I felt it is what God wanted me to do. In the time I'd known Kendrick, that was the most vulnerable he'd ever been with me and that moment truly touched my heart. My intentions were pure and there wasn't a single ulterior motive attached. Had there been, my feelings would've been crushed. Had this been me in the beginning of this situation when I was super thirsty for him, I would have drowned.

Thus bringing me to the cure: don't move unless God tells you to. From things as small as texting to something as major as a gift, do not do it without God. It sounds tedious and maybe even disheartening to some extent, but when you think of how much He protects us from, it's the best option. He knows what we need, who we need, and more importantly, who needs us. That gift for Kendrick wasn't my attempt to get in his good graces. I mean, I am a gift giver without a doubt, but I didn't get him a gift because I wanted to, I did it because I was led to. Had God not put it on my heart, it would've never been done. And I don't personally know what that gift meant to him since it was never acknowledged, but God knew what he needed and used me to provide it.

What if that man that you're thirsting over is someone that God only wants you to pour into? Has your desire to be in a relationship outweighed how God intended to use you in this situation? Imagine if God doesn't even need you to do anything for him, but to walk away so He can help him grow? Now, I'm not saying that I'm perfect, but I've been on both sides of the spectrum, and now I'm in a place where I operate on God's command and not my own. I've tried it my way and we can agree, clearly it doesn't work — and since you're reading this book, I can assume the same for you. God is the answer to the problem and the cure to thirst. Are you willing to take Him at His word? Are you okay with relinquishing that control?

THE THIRST ISN'T NEW; FIND THE ROOT

As a Life Coach, I've talked people through more issues than I can count. And while the problems were diverse in nature they all had a very distinct commonality: they all began long ago in their childhood, before manifesting in adulthood. The same can be said for you and I.

That just made you uncomfortable, didn't it? I'm sorry, but that's why we're here to get out of our comfort zones and grow, right? Right! But I'll take it easy on you for now and use myself as a prime example.

My parents had me in their very early twenties, while they were still trying to figure out what to do next, after their recent engagement. Fast forward to me being five years old, and things had drastically changed. The engagement was off, their 11-year old relationship was over, and I am now being raised by a single parent. Though, my dad was seriously the best! He picked me up every weekend and as a family, we went to Disney World for my birthday every year until I was 6. Honestly, I was the happiest kid you could ever meet.

Then things changed.

My dad had a new girlfriend and decided to attend law school several hours away. That was the beginning of the shift and it honestly never got better from there. I went from seeing him every weekend to seeing him maybe once a month. Birthdays dwindled from extravagant celebrations of my life to a quick trip to Toys 'R' Us, to a card with cash, to just a phone call. It all depreciated before my very eyes, and before you knew it, my father was no longer my 'daddy,' he was my business partner. When I needed money, I called and he would deliver what he could. From my point of view, that was enough for him, yet it was far from what I needed. But the money wasn't my goal, I just wanted my daddy back. The man who I thought could do no wrong, because he did everything perfectly. The man who spoke with intellect and authority, but could also make the best pancakes you've ever tasted. That's who was important to me, that's what that little girl needed.

Today, I'm blessed to say that I've been coached through my daddy issues and now I'm in a much better place — though, I also have to acknowledge that, that's where it all began. He is the reason why gifts don't impress me, why a man who dedicates his time grabs my attention and those who make a lackluster effort get overlooked ASAP. To this very day, my primary love language is quality time because that's all I wanted from my dad.

What did you miss as a child that you now look for in a man? Was your father absent? Did your mom make you feel like you weren't enough and now you look for validation? Did someone sexually abuse you and now you feel like sex is the only way to secure affection? Were you treated like the stepchild and now you seek the attention or approval of man?

Whatever the cause, I want you to know two things:

YOU'RE NOT ALONE. YOU CAN OVERCOME IT.

Clichés to some but I want you to take this to heart and not for the sake of my sales, but for your own integrity. You are a woman who may not have had the easiest upbringing, and though others may have had it worse, it doesn't discount what you experienced or the impact that it has had on you. Those very issues that came to mind when you read over those questions are the reasons you date the way you do. They are the cause of how you interact with people and the source of why you accept certain things too. Yes, we can blame people who've impacted us over the last few year for our issues, but we will continue to see the cycle repeated until we get to the root of why we let them occur. And please, don't be ashamed to seek counseling or therapy to work out these kinks. Trust me, you wouldn't be the first person to do so. Plus, at this point, it's not about them or him, now it's about you.

You're old enough to make the change, and mature enough to get the help you need. It doesn't make you crazy. In fact, it will take you to a level of sanity you never knew existed. Though, regardless of your next step, acknowledging the cause has to be the first.

It's not always issues with our parents, but sometimes it is. Yet, that shouldn't be an issue that you keep paying for as an adult. They did the best that they could with what they knew, in that moment, and some just didn't know at all. We've all done some things that we wouldn't mind erasing from our life, but that's not an option. Our parents are the same way. So take the time to deal with that pain.

Touching those childhood wounds may feel like some of the most unbearable moments in your life, but I promise, it will be worth it in the end. I couldn't stand hearing that deep down inside, I hated my father. Hated: a word that rarely leaves my lips, but I had to face that reality in order to make it my past. You can be set free from your pain and buried burdens too...when you're ready. Just remember that it's no longer about anyone else, this book was written for you — because I want you to be better than you were when you picked it up, but accept that you'll first have to get more uncomfortable to get there. Are you ready to get rid of your thirst and dig up its roots? Then meet me in chapter 8.

CHAPTER 8

Forgive What Seems Unforgivable

FORGIVENESS CAN BE SO bittersweet. You want to let go of whatever happened; you want to move on with life like it doesn't affect you, but you want them to be just as impacted by the memories and the pain as you are. But that's not how this thing called forgiveness works, and honestly, in order for you to make room for the person that God has for you, you have to release the toxicity of unforgiveness. Before we jump in, grab your journal (or the space provide) and prepare to begin the work needed to forgive what seems unforgivable.

SO, MY FIRST QUESTION TO YOU IS, WHO IS IT THAT YOU NEED TO FORGIVE?
"I need to forgive *[insert name]*."

_____

_____

_____

_____

_____

SECONDLY, WHAT DO YOU NEED TO FORGIVE THEM FOR?

"I need to forgive *[insert name]* for *[insert description for the pain or cause]*."

_____
_____
_____
_____

LASTLY, WHY HAVEN'T YOU ALREADY FORGIVEN THEM?

"I haven't forgiven *[insert name]* for hurting me because *[insert description of why you haven't forgiven this person]*."

_____
_____
_____
_____
_____
_____
_____
_____
_____
_____
_____
_____
_____
_____
_____
_____
_____
_____

I know, I know, you didn't come here for journal exercises on 'how to heal old wounds,' you came to read about dating! Well, believe it or not, if you never resolve those issues, you'll struggle all the more to have a healthy relationship.

That forgiveness that you're withholding, only manifests itself as negativity in your heart, and then it spills over into other areas of your life; especially in dating. Don't believe me? Okay, let's examine it: if you're struggling with daddy issues, take a look at the men you date and their habits. If your dad was absent, meaning either partially a part of your life or not around at all; I can almost assure you that you're dating men who are emotionally unavailable, inconsistent in their affections towards you, and who refuse to really make a commitment.

If you're wrestling with things related to verbal or physical abuse from your past, you're likely dealing with self-esteem issues. As a result, you date men who not only refuse to see your worth, but they also devalue you in the process — speaking to you as if you don't matter, not respecting the title that he's given you (if you have one), or let's be extremely honest, you may be a side chick (either willingly or unbeknownst to you).

I've said all of that to reiterate that when you don't forgive someone for a past hurt, it'll surface in your present decisions and relationships. And you may not like what I'm about to say, but because I love you I have to say it anyway: you're struggling in your singleness because of what you've allowed this pain to do to you, not because of the person who did it.

Let's digest that one more time.

YOU'RE STRUGGLING IN YOUR SINGLENESS BECAUSE OF WHAT YOU'VE ALLOWED THIS PAIN TO DO TO YOU, NOT BECAUSE OF THE PERSON WHO DID IT.

Yes, what happened to you is awful. No, you didn't deserve whatever he or she did. They haven't forced you to live with that burden and pain, yet, you've allowed yourself to do so. See, they are the ones who caused the wound and even helped it spread to your mind, but you are the one who allowed it to infect your life. You cannot be afraid of owning your world; the good, the bad, or the ugly and doing what needs to be done, to fix what's broken.

That process, as painful as it may feel, begins with you forgiving what seems unforgivable. Indeed, that's an oxymoron, but the power of this decision will change your entire world. Not only clearing your heart day-by-day (because it takes time to do this) but also ridding you of the desire to cope with this tragedy. What does that mean? Remember how I pointed out that what happened to you is affecting your dating life now? Well, when you heal those wounds, you stop that pattern. No more dating guys who are subconsciously your father. You learn that what resides between your legs is a precious gift, not a way to prove your worth, like the person who violated you led you to believe. I know, those wounds hurt and the scars run deep, my love, but you are literally one decision away from finally allowing scar tissue to cover the open flesh. The spirit of forgiveness is not the easiest thing that you will ever do, and I would be a liar if I told you it only takes 'x amount of days.' But what I can tell you is that you will be so much better just for beginning that journey. Yet, I must advise that while I urge you to take the steps needed to heal, I cannot force you to do so — actually, no one can. This is on you and you alone because help isn't on the way, especially since no one knows you need it.

You have to decide that you truly want it. As a Certified Life Coach, I can't tell you how many people will sign up for coaching, only to come and try to debate every step of the process. Life Coaches, therapists, psychiatrists, whichever you choose to see, all specialize in healing one way or another. Though, they can't pressure you into ripping off the band-aid to treat the wound. So, before you make an appointment and make the investment, make sure that you are ready.

ACCEPTING THE APOLOGY THAT MAY NEVER COME...

I was sexually assaulted.

Yeah, you read that correctly.

I was 18 and a guy that I once considered my best friend, swung by my house for a visit. It had been a while since we saw each other, but we did keep in touch every blue moon — so he was welcomed.

He arrived a little before sunset and we decided to talk in the car behind my front yard hedges for a little privacy, like the typical teenager. Well, as we were talking, it began to become dark outside. By this point, I'm tired and ready to call it a night, i.e. it's time for him to go. But for some reason, even with my overdramatic yawns and eye rubbing, he's not taking the hints. Like I said, it had been some time since we saw each other, so I didn't want to be rude — but we were seconds from me blurting out "alright, goodnight!" That's when all of a sudden, he's kissing me. I quickly push him away, "Ronnie, I'm not interested in us being *that* kind of friends!"

Just from the look on his face, I could see that he was in another world; not hearing me and now it's all happening so fast. He's tugging to unbutton my jeans with one hand and trying to pull my tank top down with the other, while forcing himself on me. Shocked and speechless are the only two words to describe my reaction, but they are beyond an understatement. I fight back to show that 'no, means no!' and with my breasts exposed, jeans undone, he stops dead in his tracks like he finally heard me. The look in his eyes showed me that I needed to get out of there ASAP and I did. Ronnie would go on to reach out to me for weeks, but despite his every attempt, I didn't respond. I mean, how could I?! If I didn't fight back, how would the story have ended? If I wasn't that close to my house, what would have happened to me? I can't even begin to fathom, but I thank God that imagining the 'what ifs' is all I have to do. However, instead of seeking help or running in to tell my mom what happened, I literally just went on like nothing ever happened. Like that night was a bad dream and just because I woke up, I didn't have to think about it — like it didn't leave a scar.

Fast forward to almost a year later, I'm relaxing in my dorm room and found myself doing something I'd hardly ever done — replaying that entire night, moment-by-moment — and that's when it hit me. Someone who I once called my "male best friend," a guy that knew my darkest secrets throughout my youth and who my family adored, attempted to rape me. Me. It happened to me. The thought of it all brought me to my knees and left me wailing for God. I needed Him to remove the painful yoke, to heal my heart, and to help me begin to close this wound. I cried out to my inner self to forgive myself for not trying to overcome this sooner and for dragging around this deadweight. I cried because I knew I had to forgive Ronnie. Pretending that it never happened was killing me slowly and my relationship with men had totally changed. To gain my trust was a mission and to earn my love was a fight. It wasn't easy to love me and I made it nearly impossible to let someone in to receive my love in return.

But that day, in that moment, as the pain exited my body and rolled down my cheeks for what felt like hours, I accepted the apology I had yet to receive. It was the first time I acknowledged what really happened that night. In fact, it was the first time I showed any emotion towards it at all. That burden was heavier than I ever realized and like a dam holding back raging waters, it finally broke the smile it hid behind. Not only did I begin *the process to forgive* him that day, but I also found the strength to let my emotions speak. Giving a voice to pain buried that deep, ended up being a mixture of relief and sorrow. It was like God unleashed a deep breath into my heart, melting the part of me that froze that night. I finally accepted the truth. I was finally free. I could finally feel. I finally let myself breathe.

Close to a year later, as I sat on my bed studying for an exam, Facebook chimes to tell me I have a new message. I open my inbox and you guessed it, it was a message from Ronnie. I stared at it for a while because I saw the first few lines in the preview pane. It seemed to be a regular "hey, how've you been?" message, which I could clearly do without. I was about to let my flesh rise and craft the rudest reply, but instead I thought of the progress I'd made over the last year. It would all be in vain and really, not true progress at all, if a single word from him could send me spiraling back to hate — so I took a deep breath and opened the message. It definitely began as nonchalant as it seemed from the preview, but that was his way of getting to the nitty-gritty. He went on to say he doesn't know what came over him, or why he was so aggressive and how horrible he felt for belittling me to an object instead of his friend. How it killed him to know that someone who was once his best friend in the world, was now the last person who wanted to hear his voice. While this thought never crossed my mind, as I read each word I realized he was hurting too.

See, in every multi-person encounter, we all have our own experiences, depicted from our point of view. Yet, this was the first time I became aware of the fact that we both left that night scared and in pain. Yes, we each handled it differently, but we both needed to heal

He went on to say that he never intended to hurt me and though it took a minute to sink in, he understood that no meant no. He ended it with a heartfelt apology and said that he would understand if I never spoke to him again.

That was the apology that I never thought would come. As I cried reading every word, I began to smile because not only had I truly forgiven him but I also forgave myself. Yes, myself. If I'm being honest, I walked away from that night feeling guilty, as if I did something to make him act that way. Could it have been what I wore? Was I too affectionate? So many questions flooded my mind as I probed for fault in myself, before I accepted the fact that it happened at no fault of my own. So thank God that I did the work, because it was priceless to finally know it was official — in my heart, soul, and being; **we** were both forgiven.

I know your story may not end the same as mine, but that doesn't mean you don't have the power to forgive. Notice, I didn't wait for him to apologize because I'd already decided that for my sake, he needed to be forgiven. You're probably looking at this page with a strong side eye by now, but let me just remind you of how powerful forgiveness truly is, even when the person doesn't apologize.

As Jesus hung on the cross, he was mocked, poked and prodded, to degrees much worse than the common criminal. In the last moments before his ascension to heaven, he spoke one of the last things that he would ever say before his death:

[34]Jesus said, "Father, forgive them, for they don't know what they are doing." (Luke 23:34 WEB)

Now granted, you and I are not Jesus, right? Yeah, not even close. However, that's even more of a reason why we need to work to extend forgiveness. When I think about what Jesus was going through; being beaten until he was unrecognizable and being treated like he deserved every blow, I think of how angry he must have been. I think of how he must've thought, "I'm here dying for you! Yet, you're the ones persecuting me even though I'm innocent!" And in that, I understand why He asked God to forgive them. Had they known he was truly the Messiah, the one to come and redeem the world, would they have done him this way? Not at all. But it had to happen in order for Jesus to fulfill the prophecy foretold. If the person who hurt you had the chance to look into your future, to see how much damage they would cause, would they still decide to hurt you? Maybe not. Either way, I wholeheartedly believe that "*we who are strong ought to bear the weaknesses of the weak, and not to please ourselves. (Romans 15:1 WEB)*

Our testimonies, though painful, are not only predestined to make us stronger but also to save another. However, a hurting heart can't share its truth. That's why you have to forgive the person who wronged you. It's not for them; it's for you. It's for the girl who is thinking of killing herself because she can't cope with the pain or the little boy who may become a predator when he gets older. It's for the woman who has been in a detrimental cycle all of these years — and for the aches in your heart that, that person will never be able to heal. Forgiveness is not theirs to own, it is your gift to give; even if they never know they've received it. The guards never apologized to Jesus, but he also issued forgiveness without waiting for them to.

You know, this reminds me of something my little cousin says after someone complains, "But did you die?" Rude, right? But take it into account when it comes to your life. Yeah, they hurt you, but did you die? Yes, they left you scarred, but did you die? That person may never face jail time or even utter the words "I'm sorry," but did you die? No. You're reading this book, which means not only did you not die, but you have the option to forgive and live!

Though, as I said before, it is completely up to you to decide to go forth and begin the healing process. Regardless of if you decide to or not, let me just remind you of two things:

1. FORGIVENESS IS NOT THEIRS TO OWN;
IT IS YOUR GIFT TO GIVE.
2. YOU SURVIVED IT ALL FOR A REASON, AND IT WASN'T TO WALK AROUND CARRYING THIS PAIN.

Forgive, live, and share your testimony. Someone is waiting to be saved by your strength.

CHAPTER 9

Own it!

"You're single? I'm so sorry to hear that!"
"Aww, girl. I don't know how you do it. I always keep a man."
"What?! Why are you still single?"

I could fill this entire chapter with these kinds of questions and levels of pity that we receive on a regular basis, all because of our relationship status. However, my issue isn't so much the inquiries or shame they try to cast; it's our responses. Women lower their heads, make excuses, cower behind a religious phrase, or find a way to change the topic, all because they're afraid to just say: "I am and I love it." Do you know how many people would look at you with shock?

Which reminds me of a conversation I'll never forget. I was having brunch with an old friend and one of her girlfriends (who I'd just met), and of course, dating came up.

Old friend: So...are you dating?
Me: Nope. I'm single
"Just-met'er" girl: Oh me too! But I'm always on a date. Haha!
*Me: Oh no, I date when I want to but I'm single, single. *chuckles**
Old friend: Not "single, single." Lordy!

"Just-met'er" girl: I couldn't be single, single. Girl, no. I don't know how you do it.

Giggles around the table

Me: Well, I just don't believe in wasting my time if a man isn't what I'm looking for and I have no problem with friend-zoning dudes. No need to catch feelings for someone I don't see a future with. Like, think of it this way: I go on a couple of dates a month, with quality men. I'd rather do that and enjoy my singleness with men who are at least worth some of my time, than go out every weekend with dudes who aren't worth any of it.

Silence

"Just-met'er" girl: Oh my God, I totally understand that. I always end up dating the bums! Like one dude was driving his friend's car when he took me out and then once I was sprung, he pulled up in his. Girl, it was a broke down van!

Old friend: Ha — I remember that! He waited a good minute to show you the truth. As soon as he knew you were hooked, he let the truth hang out. Haha!

Giggles

"Just-met'er" girl: But like, honestly, I just want to get married. You don't think about the fact that we're getting older? Or want to hurry up and have kids?

Me: Ha! Girl, who doesn't? But I don't want to rush into a marriage just to end up hoping for a divorce. Plus, I'm just trying to make sure my desires don't trump God's plans — so I'll take my time, learn whatever I need to learn about 'me,' and do what I need to do to fulfill my purpose in this season — because even though I'd love for it to be right now, my main goal is for it to be right.

Old friend: Hmm, I hear that! I wish I would've waited and paid attention to the signs. I wouldn't be getting divorced now.

"Just-met'er" girl: Hmm...

Silence

At that moment, I could've easily given in to the pressure and tried to make an excuse for my singleness. Yet, I would have failed the truth, myself, everything I believe in, this book, and you, if I had.

This book was inspired by conversations just like that one, where women felt rushed and pressured into settling for anything just to have something. I decided to write this book because of countless phone calls where my friends were telling me how they were settling for a piece of a man, just to say they had one. I wrote this book because God tasked me with reminding you of your worth and dignity.

You know, in my heart of hearts and to the deepest part of my soul, I feel like our purpose really unfolds in phases. And as a single lady, you have the time to give to Him your undivided attention. Meaning, while you are single, there is work for you to do! God hasn't kept you single as a punishment; He's allowed it because, in this season, there is a prize. No, it doesn't consist of you sitting around waiting for "Boaz," so get off Yoaz and get it done. (Wait, that shocked you. Okay, now I need to ice the wound) I LOVE YOU!! (I'm hugging you. Feel it? Okay, good.)

Woo, that was a lot, huh? But it was so necessary. I've met girls on their way to obtaining impressive degrees, phenomenal careers or businesses, and with the brightest futures ahead of them and all they can think about is how dreadful it is to be single.

Girl, what?!

No, ma'am, it's not dreadful, it's amazing. It means you aren't willing to settle and you know what? It also implies that God loves you enough to work on your man before you meet him. So no, it's not something to cower about; be "single, single" and be proud of that badge! Wear it with honor and wear it with the knowledge that you will one day be the wife and mother (if you aren't already, a mommy) if you truly desire and are destined to be. Trust me, God sees the breakups, the heartache, the frustration, the tears, and the lonely nights — and

He's keeping track because, at the appointed time, He will give you beauty for those ashes. [Isaiah 61:1-3 WEB]

But, before He does, you have to truly walk in this season like you really do own it. Which means, be confident enough to say you are single and don't feel ashamed when people belittle that status. You're here for a reason, find out what that is and make the best of it! There is nothing more depressing than seeing a woman full of potential wasting away because she's focused on what she doesn't have. Get out of that constant state of lack and begin to focus on the areas where you're experiencing abundance.

YOU ARE BEAUTIFUL, YOU'RE A BOSS,
YOU'RE A QUEEN, YOU ARE AN INTELLECTUAL,
YOU'RE WELL TRAVELED, YOU'RE CULTURED,
YOU'RE ADVENTUROUS, YOU ARE VIRTUOUS,
YOU ARE WINNING, YOU LACK NOTHING,
YOU'RE BLESSED, YOU ARE CALLED,
YOU'RE A GIFT, YOU'RE GREATNESS,
YOU ARE POWERFUL BEYOND MEASURE,
AND YOU ARE GOD'S.

Own every, single, ounce of all of the above. It's who **you** are. And if you feel like you can't relate to that list, write your own! But never give in to the notion that you aren't amazing. Never assume that because you don't have what society thinks you should, that you're missing something. God promised to provide for you in all areas and based on the mere fact that you're reading this book, I can tell you that He has. He may not give you everything that you want, but He has never missed the chance to provide you with what you need. You are His daughter, and right now, you are completely His because you are single. That's beautiful, love. Own it.

CHAPTER 10

Breaking Soul-ties

B EFORE WE BEGIN, PLEASE make sure you're reading this alone or at least in a quiet place. We'll do a few exercises in this chapter that'll require you to focus on your emotions and pray (or meditate) without interruption.

Alright! Let's go.

So we've all heard the term soul-tie used before, but here's how I define it:

Soul · tie (/sōl/·/tī/): a connection created between two people in the spiritual realm, when they become deeply intimate on an emotional, mental, spiritual, and or physical level.

As we date, we end up making soul-ties with several people, some of which we should've never been attached to in the first place, yet we find ourselves impacted by these ties in some way, shape or form. Thanks to these connections it ends up taking what feels like forever to get over the person or situation and thoughts of how great things used-to-be replay in your mind, all while the reasons things ended seem to be far from memory. Soul-ties.

You know he's not for you, yet you'd rather deal with the monster that you know instead of the one you don't — regardless of your family and friends urging you to let go. Soul-ties.

You finally had the courage to walk away, but you miss having someone to spend time with and the fun dates. So even without him making an effort to come back, you're debating on giving it another chance. Soul-ties.

Now let's be really transparent, you realized months ago that he wasn't ready to commit, but you're still sleeping with him, hoping he'll change his mind. He won't. Soul-ties.

He cheated on you, lied to you, and made you feel as if it was all a result of something you did or didn't do. Yet, a part of you still wants him back. Why? Soul-ties.

You haven't spoken to him in months, and he is not the least bit concerned about how you're doing. Though, you still find a reason to text him every blue moon to check on him. Soul-ties.

If you didn't relate to any of the above it's cool, because we both know you have your own story to tell. And while these soul-ties impact each of us differently, it doesn't take away from the fact that they affect us eventually. All of which stems from us letting someone in and giving them an opportunity to know us. So tell me, who *knows* you?

WHO KNOWS YOU?

We hear "he knew her" in the bible time and time again. The phrase depicts the consummation of a marriage or just to identify sex, in various situations. The first mention of it is when Adam and Eve got married, in Genesis 4:1.

In my opinion, sex is one of the deepest forms of intimacy (a.k.a "into-me-you-see"). Now regardless of how you feel about sex, it is truly one of the most vulnerable moments you'll ever experience with another. "And the two became one" is not just another biblical phrase, it actually depicts what happens when you engage in intercourse. Your body is completely open to penetration from the physical and spiritual sense. You're united with this person, you are intertwined with them, you are physically conjoined until it's over. The only physical connection that runs deeper than this is when a woman is pregnant.

Think about that for a moment. Think of how many men (and in some cases, women) have been that engulfed within your very being to where they now *know* you. In many cases, they didn't care for you, let alone love you, yet they got the chance to *know* you. They didn't concern themselves with your health enough to wear protection to help prevent pregnancy or to decrease the chances of passing on an STD, but they were blessed to *know* you. They haven't checked on you since it all went down or maintained any type of relationship worth noting, however, they can tell any and everyone that they *know* you.

And for those of you who were sexually abused, I am so sorry that someone forced themselves into your sacred space and got to *know* you without permission. You didn't deserve that and I wish it would've never happened to you. But I thank God that it didn't break you. Yes, you may still deal with the pain or remnants of what occurred, but you're better than it and stronger because of it. Thank you for fighting to survive and thank you for not giving up on love. I pray you're given beauty for your ashes sooner than later, love.

Okay, I got a little emotional typing that. Let's take a quick moment to breathe.

Now that everyone you've had some level of intimacy with are at the forefront of your mind — think of the soul- ties that are attached to you, from them. This isn't me judging your number of sexual partners, it's me giving you perspective on how many times we've all created these unbelievably strong connections. Pause. Please keep in mind, there's nothing to be ashamed of. God knew of the rough patches on your path to this day and the choices you'd make, long before you made them — and still decided to love you. He also decided to give you a way to break those chains.

So for the rest of this chapter, let's talk about how to sever these ties once and for all.

IDENTIFY THE TIE

Would your doctor treat you for a disease if you can't explain the symptoms? No, which is the same reason we're going to take a moment to identify the ties entangled with your soul.

First thing's, first: grab your journal.

Now think of the people that you've slept with or who have slept with you — and not just through vaginal intercourse. Think of the people you've had oral sex with, who you may have stopped short of sex with, and anyone who may have violated you sexually. Write their name(s) down.

_____

_____

_____

_____

_____

_____

_____

_____

_____

_____

_____

_____

_____

_____

_____

_____

_____

Remember my definition of a soul-tie?

Soul · tie (/sōl/·/tī/): a connection created between two people in the spiritual realm, when they become deeply intimate on an emotional, mental, spiritual, and or physical (via sexual intercourse) level.

As you can see, I don't believe that sex is the only way to create soul-ties. With that in mind, recall the names of those you've connected with emotionally, mentally, or spiritually that have deeply hurt you — yes, they count too. And don't fool yourself, it won't take a long time or a ton of soul searching to do find them. You know who's hurt you, we all do. Even if you're over it, they don't acknowledge it or know that they have. Go ahead and write their name(s) down too.

Look over that list and take a few minutes just to engage in as many deep breaths as you need.

BLESS THEM

This is honestly just as hard as letting it go, in some cases. But I want you to sew what you desire to reap. You deserve happiness, joy, and unwavering favor. Plant those very things in order to see them manifest in your life. Go down this list person-by-person and say a blessing over their life. I want this to be in your own words, but here's an example if you need one:

"Lord, I bless [insert name], wherever they may be and whoever they may be with. Cover their choices with your mercy and allow [insert name] to feel Your love and experience Your favor in ways they never have before, while their path leads them closer to You. In Jesus' name, I pray. Amen."

Again, this may not be easy, so take your time here.

BREAK THE TIE

Now that we've defined the tie, identified who you're tied to, and blessed them, it's time to sever the connection. This is really where I need you to be in a quiet space, where you won't be interrupted. When I completed this process, it was extremely emotional for me, yet one of the most freeing acts I've ever committed. I pray your experience is just as liberating.

Breathe.

Grab that list of names (if it's no longer in front of you).

Breathe.

Look it over.

Take a deep breath.

Pray for God to give you the words to make this impactful and for Him to truly break these bonds. Again, I want this to be in your own words because just as God speaks to us in ways we understand, your authentic prayer lingo is what God expects to hear from you. Here's an example though, just in case:

*"Abba Father, You know why I'm here and what I'm about to do. I come right now asking You to make this moment impact my dating life in the best ways possible. Give me the words to speak Holy Spirit, Lord, guide my tongue and show me how to break the bonds that I no longer want to have attached. Lead me to clear my heart, mind, and spirit, from the connections to those who **know** me. Make this moment set me on the path to be complete and whole without any missing pieces. You made me. You can restore me. You love me. I love you. So I'm asking You to lead me. Thank You for the power of the tongue that's about to set me free. In Jesus' name, I pray. Amen."*

Breathe.

Grab your list — it's declaration time.

This is part is written out for you, but as always please, speak whatever God puts on *your* heart. He knows what you need to say to make this impactful for your journey and you already prayed for Him to show you how, so by all means, follow His lead.

"Abba Father, I come before you right now, thanking You for the ability to break soul-ties. God, these ties joined to my spirit are no longer

welcomed within any fiber of my being. God right now, I release these ties and cast them away from me as far as the East is from the West. Right now, in the name of Jesus, I break the bond between me and [insert name]. Right now, in the name of Jesus, I break the bond between me and [insert name] **(repeat this as many times as needed).** *I take ownership of every fiber of my being back from all of those people and situations I just spoke. I remove them from my mind. I remove them from my heart. I remove them from my body. I remove them soul, I remove them from spirit! Father God, I proclaim that You will fill the voids that have been left from any part of me that has been given away or taken. It is only with Your love that those spaces can be filled — so I deem them full. I am filled with You. You created me and I am forever whole! I decree and declare that these soul-ties are completely broken and are to never to be re-established. I am whole! In Jesus' name, I am free!"*

Breathe!

This is such a huge and imperative step in the right direction. Those people may never be aware of the fact that they've been released, but you will see and feel the difference. You're a whole person, filled with the love of God and whom God loves beyond what you could ever imagine! You're now set free from what is behind you and deserve all that He's sending your way, my love. Own that and move forward with confidence. Go out there and Date with even more Dignity than ever before!

CHAPTER 11

Dating with Dignity

O NE DAY, I WAS on the phone with one of my closest friends (let's call her Tiffany), and we were discussing a mutual friend's, new man.

Now, for those who don't follow me on social media, let me tell you; I love, love! And whenever a new relationship manifests, people post their engagements, get married, just anything around love, I immediately turn into mush.

So, imagine my reaction when Tiffany shared the great news of how this particular friend, who had been a fellow single hopeful-romantic, had a new relationship. I was elated! Though, being that Tiffany is one of my best friends, she let me know that all that glittered wasn't exactly gold. My excitement slowly dwindled as she began to tell me some of the things this dude was putting our friend through and needless to say, my mushy mode went from 100 to 0, real quick. Before I knew it, I was on the edge of my bed with my face in my palms ready to cry.

"She's so amazing, Tiff — why in the hell would she put up with all of that?!"

Then it hit me; she didn't know her worth. She wanted to be in a relationship so bad that she let this dude slide into a spot he didn't deserve. She was doing what we've all done and that's dating without much dignity. I wasn't floored by her situation, but I knew she was one of many. I've been her and since you're reading this book, I think it's safe to assume you have too. With that heavily on my heart, God put it in my spirit to use my thoughts, lessons, and wisdom from my personal experiences, to create the pages that you now hold.

Now, you know why I took the time to write this book. It was never about the book deal or the money that will come. It was always about you. I want to see women rise above the common decision to settle, heal their wounds, and walk with integrity, like nothing the world has witnessed before. The goal is to ensure that you date and eventually (if it's destined) marry, with dignity.

With that in mind, I wanted to use this chapter to share several lessons that I've learned, which can help keep both of us focused on our standards and give us the freedom to never again date blindly and out of an insecure place. So, go ahead and grab your highlighter; class is back in session!

DESPERATE = DISASTER

So you know that guy who's saying all of the right things and may even look like your type. The one who makes you blush but also shows red flags with every interaction? We both know he's clearly not for you for several reasons; so he needs to go, ASAP. Not because I think he's awful but because I know you're worth so much more and deserve God's best for you. I mean really, is he the man you imagined being with or is he just enough man to keep your panties wet? Oops, you didn't expect that, did you? Sorry, I ain't sorry, because the truth of the matter is you're only dating him because you're desperate and losing faith in God's timing. It's okay, I'm not judging where you are — I just love you too much to leave you there.

Imagine the man of your dreams really coming through at this very moment. Approaching you with all of the right qualities, the credentials, and the Godliness you desire. You're saying to yourself that you'd be happy and would definitely be ready to be his woman, but the reality is, you're so preoccupied with someone who isn't supposed to be there, that you won't even notice him. No, I don't think you should be a spinster and sit around to rot until Kingdom comes, but becoming completely committed to someone who you know isn't the one, isn't ideal either. That's what desperation does to us! It blocks our hope for the future, making us feel like it's now or never, and it's all such a lie. I refuse to believe that God would deliver you from some of the most traumatizing moments anyone could ever survive; from molestation, to rape, to verbal and physical abuse, miscarriages, cancer, so on and so forth — just to have you settle.

You're an award all by yourself and you should feel like you won gold in your relationship; not the basic participation prize. Be bold enough to look that man (aka all of your desperation) in the face and tell him it's time to go. Be brave enough to fight for what you deserve and if that's not enough motivation, be determined enough to fight for you. You've come too far and survived too much to give up on any facet of your life now. You deserve to win in every area, but especially in love.

KEEP YOUR EYES OFF THEM!

They have the kids, the house, the careers, the looks, and maybe even the fame — #RelationshipGoals! Gosh, you love "them" so much that you can't even acknowledge anyone that doesn't fit into the plan you've created to mimic their life. But what did it take for them to get there? What struggles did they have to overcome to see the fruit of their labor? Yeah, you won't see that in your timeline. Though, if they're real, they will tell you they aren't perfect. Think about all of the celebrity relationships that you once idolized, that are now just a distant memory for social media and them. Why? Because it didn't work. Which doesn't bother me, that's life, right? Not everything is meant to last, and not all relationships will stand the test of time, but the one that you're believing God for will — if you stop trying to create it based on what you see. You don't know what your husband looks like and you don't know what trials will come with the blessing of a new relationship, but you will know Who brought it together. You'll know that it wasn't destined to fall apart and that even when things get tough, He determined that you two will win. In this season of singleness, you have to learn to walk by faith and not by sight, because what God has for you is not something that you've seen before. Trust that and stop looking to recreate someone else's marriage. God is exceptionally creative and has yet to run out of ideas on how to uniquely bless us all. I promise.

NEVER GIVE IN

Some of you have been single for a week or a month, while others have been in this place for years. No need to bash or feel sorry for either end of the spectrum, because the truth is, we all are on a similar journey, traveling the single seas. And just because we aren't in the exact same place, doesn't mean that I can't empathize with how tired you may be. So trust me when I say, you're not alone — which is even more of a reason not to give in. We're all working on ourselves, exercising our faith day-by-day, and believing in God's timing with every new sun and moon.

And while many of us are on this journey, I want to take a moment to point out the bystanders on the brink watching too. Some are cheering you on and others are waiting to see you fail. No matter their stance, you are a walking testament to them. They hear you talk about waiting on God and if they don't know Him for personally, they're waiting to see if He'll deliver — which is cool...until *you* give up, give in, and settle. That wasn't a part of His plan, and yet, that becomes what they see as the result of your prayers. Doesn't that sound awful? A solid chance to minister to someone without even saying a word, just by simply living out what you believe — ruined, because you decided to stop trusting God. We both know that's not what you want because, deep down, you know it's not worth the gamble.

Think of every time you've read of God blessing someone in the bible, it habitually involved a wait. You've seen Him blow your mind and come through in the clutch before, so you know He can do it again. But are you willing to wait? If so, stand firm in that decision and embrace it. Re-read chapter 9 and a few others to get the courage to own it! You deserve His best and come hell or high waters, know that He intends to make sure you experience it. But you can't give up and I urge you not to give in.

WATCH WHO YOU CALL A FRIEND

Friend: a word that gets tossed around as common as the word 'love' but carries very little respect and at times, even less weight. This is a book about dating, but I think it's imperative to mention that watching who you call a friend in this process is just as crucial as Dating with Dignity. We all have close friends and we have associates. There's a vast difference in the two, but what I want to caution here is not the differentiating definitions, but actions. You will want to vent about this process to someone, so make sure that whomever you talk to is truly a trusted confidant, that's leading you closer to God for clarity and giving wise counsel.

Look over your sister-circle and choose your community carefully, pray for God to remove those who are not wholeheartedly wishing you the best, and for Him to help those harboring even the slightest bit of jealousy or judgment. Can't see someone being jealous? Well, while you may see your singleness as a disaster area, there is always someone who sees you and wishes that disaster was theirs. So all-in-all, hone in on your discernment as you build and spill to your community. Your

God-given friends and family will be there to help you through this process, and truly, you'll need it — just be mindful of who you invite to witness.

FORGIVE YOURSELF

It's easy to think about all that you have done wrong up to this point — the things that God may be currently "punishing" you for. But if you've read the Bible, you know what I'm about to say. Based on Hebrews 8:12, you're forgiven. Though, if we're being honest, that's not really the part that you're struggling with. You accept that God forgives you and not *really* counting your sins against you anymore. The tough part is that you haven't forgiven yourself. Again, I'm not judging you. I'm speaking from experience.

This is an ever-changing process. We are ever-changing people. We never stop growing, we never stop learning, we never stop getting it right and wrong — meaning, we'll *always* have to remember to forgive ourselves. There are entire sections in this book dedicated to forgiving others and I'm sure there'll be one on forgiving yourself in the second one. But don't wait for me, I need you to start now. Doing so levels your thoughts and helps you realize that you're not perfect and gives you the grace and space needed to be better, moving forward. Embrace your faults and failures.

As a matter of fact, grab your journal: I dare you to make a bulleted list of the ones that currently plaguing your mind. Then, write the lesson you've learned from that fault or failure.

FAILURE _____

LESSON_____

_____

FAILURE _____

LESSON_____

_____

FAILURE _____

LESSON_____

_____

FAILURE _____

LESSON_____

_____

Lastly, write an uplifting note to yourself based on the lessons.

MY NOTE TO SELF

You're confident enough not to settle. You're too amazing to be option #2. You're worth waiting for and what you desire is too. Trust God in this process and don't let anything lower your standards. You deserve greatness girly...and it's coming. - Me

Now keep that note on you from now on, and every time you feel the guilt or the enemy attacking you with thoughts of what was, look at how God turned that problem into a blessing for your good. Take a moment to do the same. Own your mistakes, faults, and failures. Give yourself permission to not be picture perfect and enjoy the freedom that comes with that peace. It's priceless.

ATTACK YOUR ISSUES, HEAD-ON

I had trust issues.

I used to think they were stemming from the dudes I was dating but even after being cheated on, I decided to do a little soul-searching to find the real root. From that, I learned my trust issues weren't just from my dating choices but were rooted in memories from men I'd watched all of my life.

They were from witnessing infidelity left and right, as a child. From abandonment issues I'd never addressed and from being let down when I needed someone the most. Issues.

We run from them until we can't. They haunt us in more ways than one and leave us finding excuses for everything that's happening around us, damning the people we feel like are making it happen to us, and all the while, not realizing the real problems are within us. Issues.

I realized that many times those issues were attracting the very type of man that I didn't want to be with. That doesn't have to be your story. It's not too late. You can attack your stumbling blocks through therapy, life coaching, counseling, whatever feels best for you. But don't ignore them and whatever you do, don't let them go untreated. You're phenomenal and more valuable than you know, but these issues are like a disease.

They don't seem to cause any trouble until they're affecting everything that's within you and disrupting what's happening around you. The symptoms surface when something triggers them and for me, my trigger was commitment. The closer my dating situation got to becoming serious, the more I began to question if he was ready to commit at all. I've ruined some great relationships running from my issues and even more by ignoring them. But you don't have to allow your inner struggles to play you like a puppet — own and attack them head-on, the best way you can. Your life will be so much more peaceful and fulfilled when you do, and you deserve every ounce of that too.

STOP EXPECTING PERFECTION

We are all human and we're all extremely flawed. Even the guys in the Bible had issues: Moses was a drunk, David was an adulterer, Abraham was a liar and the list goes on. No one was perfect and no one is perfect. You are not perfect. So then, why do we expect perfection from every relationship? Why do we want to run when things get tough or when it doesn't fit the fairytale we've imagined?

It's because we aren't realistic and don't allow others to simply be who they are. It's because we date people who don't truly meet our standards and then get upset when they don't eventually rise to them. We're conditioned to expect people to fit into a mold we created based on what we want our lives to look like. It's unfair, unhealthy, and will leave you disappointed every time. The good news is, as you work on the other items previously noted, this unrealistic expectation becomes less of a "law" in your life, and you end up free from the story you've envisioned. Imagine how smoothly your life would flow if you truly let go and let God? Think of how many blessings you've turned into curses because it didn't look the way you wanted it to. Break free of that cycle that leaves you cynically trying to predict and manipulate every situation with those you love. Learn to love the people in your life for who they are, not who you want them to be. In doing this, by releasing the need for your life to be perfect, you will finally be free.

WHERE IS YOUR TRUST?

When we get into a relationship, we tend to put a lot of trust in that person. Yet, that's the last place where our trust should reside. God is the only consistent in our lives and He is the only One who has our best interest at heart, every second of every day. Man is finicky, man is unreliable, man is emotional, man gets spiritually attacked, man is made of flesh, man is not perfect, and man is a man. None of us are without fault or sin and we can be selfish without realizing it — so ask yourself, is that really where your trust should reside?

I have a friend who's happily married and one day while we were talking about relationships, she said *"Ces, I don't trust that my husband will never cheat. He's human. But I trust that the God in Him would give him the strength not to."* Wow!

Imagine trusting the Holy Spirit to convict them when a wrong thought crosses their mind? Think of the amount of peace in trusting that the God in them will help control their lustful desires. God wants to bless you with insurmountable freedom in this area. But are you willing to put your trust in His hands through every season of your love life?

DON'T GET LOST LIKE LEAH

Do you remember Leah? In essence, the Bible describes her as Jacob's unwanted wife [Genesis 29:15-35 WEB]. As the scriptures tell us, Jacob was in love with a woman named Rachel and worked for her father Laban to earn her hand in marriage. But instead of being an honest man, Laban tricked Jacob and decided to marry off his eldest daughter, Leah, instead of Rachel, as he'd promised. Leah, a woman with "weak eyes," a full heart, and a desire to be loved, did all that she could to be the best wife possible. Jacob eventually marries Rachel but while she lay barren, Leah was blessed to birth multiple children — and ultimately is listed a part of Jesus' lineage. Though, in Genesis 29, the Bible notes that after each child, she continually praises God because all she could think is *now my husband will love me.*" It's not until she gives birth to her last child, Judah, that we see a change in perspective:

> [35]*She conceived again, and bore a son. She said, "This time will I praise Yahweh." Therefore she named him Judah. Then she stopped bearing. (Genesis 29:35)*

In dating, after seeing what I've seen and in learning what I've learned, I completely understand how so many of us become lost like Leah.

We get into something special and we thank God for this great thing that He has done. We smile because it's new, fresh, and we're beaming with that "I've gotta new babe," glow. But somewhere in there, we tend to forget Who put it together and oftentimes, who we were before it began.

For the sake of transparency, I'll admit I've broken the cardinal rule in dating: I made "him" an idol and ended up pushing God to the back burner. We know that God is a jealous God and even if He blesses us with the man of our dreams, He'll gladly remove him if he begins to trump God's place in our hearts. He'll even be swift to break it up the minute we start to make our "new boo" a priority over His purpose. God never intends for us to totally fail in anything and will only let us go so far down the road of destruction, before attempting to get our attention. Leah had several kids before she realized what God was waiting for her to see: no matter how her husband made her feel, He'd always loved her, wanted to bless her, and had a greater purpose for her. When she changed her perspective and came to this realization, she stopped conceiving.

What are you continually giving birth to because you refuse to acknowledge God? Hurt? Pain? Rejection? It's not His will that anyone called by His name should perish [2 Peter 3:9], but if you refuse to fix your eyes on Him, He can't show you a way out. We get so lost in the hunt for "love" that we neglect His love. And truth be told, any man that isn't pointing you back to God is not the man for you. Pray for God to give you eyes to see His will and wisdom to trust His plan for your life. Give it all to God and refuse to remain lost, habitually birthing things with the wrong motives. Let go and become found like Leah, when you finally give God His due.

Pause. Breathe. That was a lot.

ACCEPT THAT YOU CAN'T CHANGE "JON."

Meet Jon.

Jon has a Ph.D. brings home a six-figure salary from his 9-5, owns a consulting firm on the side, drives a top of the line car, dresses like he's fresh off the pages of GQ, has rugged good looks, plays golf, loves poetry, hip-hop, and cuddling.

I can hear you over there saying, *"Hey, Jon!"*

Jon also has four kids that he doesn't take care of, a small gambling problem, spends excessively and will cheat on you every chance he gets.

Oh, now you don't want Jon?

The sad part is, there are so many women who would date Jon in a heartbeat and try to make him hubby. She'll accept his "flaws and all" and will do so with the "I can change him" mindset. Take it from someone who's dated "Jon," no matter how good of a woman you are, you can't change who he is.

Now, granted, no one is perfect, we're all a work in progress and God knows our hearts. Though, even with all of those truths, a ton of you still settle for the ultimate lie. You think that a title or wedding band will cure all of the issues that you've had with him, cause him to straighten up, and transform him into the man of your dreams. Nope, that's not how this works. You get who you get. The super sexy "Jon" that doesn't take care of his kids and cheats on you, while gambling — is still going to be "Jon" that doesn't take care of his kids and cheats on you, while gambling. Point being, when you date and or marry someone, you commit to them for who they are at that moment. It's almost like that "you break it, you buy it" theory, in relationship form. When you get into a serious relationship, make sure you're 100% okay with that person as they are, because the likelihood of them changing completely, is slim to none.

You would never date a "Jon," you say?

Remember that time you went on a date with that one guy who had you pay, even though he asked you out? Meet Jon. Oh, and what about the guy who doesn't have any kids, but he's out here practicing his baby making technique every time he cheats on you? Meet Jon. And my favorite, the guy who is cool with just having you chill at his place or hanging out at yours, but never wants to go out in public or post about your relationship online. Hey, Jon!

See, regardless of the form that he comes in, there are "Jon's" everywhere and sadly, we each have dated at least one. And there are phenomenal lessons to be learned in dating this kind of man — the most valuable being that you deserve more. You deserve who and what God has for you. He may not come with a Ph.D. and a six-figure salary, but he will come with a pure heart ready to love you with every fiber of his being, equipped with what you need now, and what God knows you'll need in the future. Most importantly, he'll come ready to claim his throne. So please, put your crown back on and kick "Jon" out! God is sending you a King, so let's say adios to that peasant.

SPEAK WHAT YOU SEEK

This is not the same thing as having a list. Take the time to sit with God and truly make your requests known, for example: "God, I desire a healthy, whole, unconditionally loving relationship with a man who is truly Yours..." The Bible tells us to listen to God, then to write the vision and make it plain [Habakkuk 2:2-3 WEB] — and the same applies here. Not because God needs your directions but because these desires need to be ingrained within you so that you're able to finally stop accepting anything less than His best for you. If you want a man who knows God, stop dating dudes who refuse to be in His presence. If you want to be in a healthy relationship, stop talking to the guys who are inconsistent. Speak what you seek! And after you've become clear in that, end with the seal that will cover you no matter what: "Father, not my will, but Your will be done." This is not to say that God won't give you what you desire. Instead, it unbinds His hands and allows Him to bless you with what you deserve. Trust me. He's got you covered.

HOLD TO YOUR VALUES

I'm far from perfect and I'm not a virgin — though, I can tell you celibacy has probably saved me from more than I could comprehend. Which leaves me to urge you, not to compromise your walk for anyone or anything. Be bold and set boundaries that don't put your weaknesses to the test. We aren't always as strong as we portray and when we become intimate with someone (on any level), it makes it that much harder to resist or even walk away. And please don't say it's the enemy looking for a moment to sneak in, we both know it's your flesh looking for a chance to show out. Be wise and be real. You know your triggers, ask him for his; set parameters that protect the sanctity of your promise to God, and move forward in knowing that He honors you when you honor Him. Don't set yourself up and don't fall short because you didn't plan to succeed. Don't trust your flesh when it says, "we can *just* do this and it'll be cool." Think back over your life, has that ever set you up for a win? Right, mine hasn't either.

THINK LIKE A LADY, ACT LIKE CHRIST

Straight no chaser — you're the daughter of the Highest. He sent His only begotten Son to the cross and endured the pain of watching Jesus die and rise again, just for you. So, why are walking around like you're worth nothing? Why are you letting dudes penetrate your virtue, literally and emotionally?

Did God not set you apart? Didn't He say you're worth more than rubies? He called you fearfully and wonderfully made — yet, you're acting as if there's nothing special about you.

Ma'am there is, you are amazing! You're gorgeous. You're a Queen. A woman called to embody the characteristics of Christ, to show the world that you are His hands and feet in modern times. No, that doesn't mean you have to be flawless, but it implies that you're not excused for acting out either.

Wear confidence every day, knowing that you are a treasure. Walk with your head held high, recognizing that you're not the average chick. Don't feel bad for having standards or wanting more out of a relationship, because you should! You're a rare woman and you deserve to be treated as such — so, continue to think like a lady, while you act like Christ.

CHAPTER 12

I Think You're Ready

'M LITERALLY SITTING IN a coffee shop, in Atlanta, floored by the fact that I'm done with this book. This is my baby, my first gift to the world, a true labor of love. A direct order from God laid on my heart years ago. I obeyed.

And while I'll always admit that I definitely do not know it all, I know Who does. So, everything between the cover until these very last pages is really His gift to you. My heart was full writing Dating with Dignity because I feel like God Himself, is tired of seeing you hurt in this season. He wanted you to know it's not a curse and that He hasn't forgotten about you, in the least bit. I'm in year 7 of true singleness while someone may be in year 20, and another is in week one. Regardless of where we stand, I know that He still has a plan. I hope you move forward in dating during this time, trusting Him and everything that He desires to bring your way. If not for anything else, for the mere fact that God is not a man, so He can't lie. If He said it, He meant it, and if He meant it, He'll do it — at the appropriate time.

No, this book won't save you from the lessons that He has for you to learn, but it's a start to transforming your heart and perspective, which in the end, makes you an intentional dater. It's such a beautiful metamorphosis.

Gosh, I don't even know your name, but I am so proud of you. I mean, I'm literally tearing up right now, because I think of how precious you are to God, that He would task me with a book, just to give you the confidence that you need in order to prepare you for what He has in store. He'd move heaven and earth, just to get a message to you and He'd literally relocate a woman from Orlando to Atlanta, just so that she could focus on writing this love letter to His daughter. If that's not enough, think of the fact that I had to go through a ton of lessons just to share wisdom from my experiences... all for you; because He loves you that much. [Romans 15:1]

Every heartache, every tear, every "Jon" and great guy (who wasn't for me) that I've dated, was for you. Not because you're weak, but because He wanted you to know you weren't alone and more importantly, He wanted you to shift your mindset. This is my first book, so I was nervous that I wouldn't be able to adequately convey that goal. Then, I remembered Who gave me this task in the first place. It'll touch who it needs to touch, bless who it's called to bless, heal who was once wounded and revive patience in the one who's losing faith. It's all for you.

That's why I call you "love." Not because I needed a clever way to address you, but because this is written to you in love. The love of Christ, to be exact. It may be harsh at times, and even corny, but as I said, God and I love you as you are, but we still love you too much to leave you there. We love you beyond who hurt you and more than what tried to break you. Yeah, you're flawed, but you're also fierce at the same time. Yes, you are a work in progress, but love, you're progressing. Oh and yes, you definitely are a bit much at times, yet He made a man who's going to love that about you too. It all boils back down to love. Love, I love you. God loves you. You are the product of love. Not just from your parents, but from the One who calls you His.

I hope you feel every ounce of that, and I pray you embrace it with open arms.

Hmm, yeah, I think you're really ready.

Have fun out there and be safe, my love.

SCRIPTURE REFERENCES

SONG OF SOLOMON 4:7 WEB | page 9

You are all beautiful, my love. There is no spot in you.

RUTH 2:1-3 WEB | page 23

[1] Naomi had a relative of her husband's, a mighty man of wealth, of the family of Elimelech, and his name was Boaz. [2] Ruth the Moabitess said to Naomi, "Let me now go to the field, and glean among the ears of grain after him in whose sight I find favor."She said to her, "Go, my daughter." [3] She went, and came and gleaned in the field after the reapers; and she happened to come to the portion of the field belonging to Boaz, who was of the family of Elimelech.

RUTH 4:5-11 WEB | page 26

[5] Then Boaz said, "On the day you buy the field from the hand of Naomi, you must buy it also from Ruth the Moabitess, the wife of the dead, to raise up the name of the dead on his inheritance." [6] The near kinsman said, "I can't redeem it for myself, lest I endanger my own inheritance. Take my right of redemption for yourself; for I can't redeem it." [7] Now, this was the custom in former time in Israel concerning redeeming and concerning exchanging, to confirm all things: a man took off his shoe and gave it to his neighbor, and this was the way of legalizing transactions in Israel. [8] So the near kinsman said to Boaz, "Buy it for yourself," then he took off his shoe. [9] Boaz said to the elders, and to all the people, "You are witnesses today, that I have bought all that was Elimelech's, and all that was Chilion's and Mahlon's, from the hand of Naomi. [10] Moreover Ruth the Moabitess, the wife of Mahlon, I have purchased to be my wife, to raise up the name of the dead on his inheritance, that the name of the dead may not be cut off from among his brothers, and from the gate of his place. You are witnesses today." [11] All the people who were in the gate, and the elders, said, "We are witnesses. May Yahweh

make the woman who has come into your house like Rachel and like Leah, which both built the house of Israel; and treat you worthily in Ephrathah, and be famous in Bethlehem.

LUKE 23:34 WEB | page 60

Jesus said, "Father, forgive them, for they don't know what they are doing."

ROMANS 15:1 WEB | page 61 & page 92

Now we who are strong ought to bear the weaknesses of the weak, and not to please ourselves.

ISAIAH 61:1-3 WEB | page 66

[1] The Lord Yahweh's Spirit is on me; because Yahweh has anointed me to preach good news to the humble. He has sent me to bind up the brokenhearted, to proclaim liberty to the captives, and release to those who are bound; [2] to proclaim the year of Yahweh's favor, and the day of vengeance of our God; to comfort all who mourn; [3] to provide for those who mourn in Zion, to give to them a garland for ashes, the oil of joy for mourning, the garment of praise for the spirit of heaviness; that they may be called trees of righteousness, the planting of Yahweh, that he may be glorified.

GENESIS 29:35 WEB | page 84

She conceived again and bore a son. She said, "This time will I praise Yahweh." Therefore she named him Judah. Then she stopped bearing.

HABAKKUK 2:2-3 WEB | page 87

[2] Then the Lord replied: "Write down the revelation and make it plain on tablets so that a herald may run with it. [3] For the revelation awaits an appointed time; it speaks of the end and will not prove false. Though it linger, wait for it; it will certainly come and will not delay.

MEET THE AUTHOR

Your Single Life Liaison

CESLY BURGESS is a motivational speaker, blogger, and natural encourager. A proud Floridan, born and raised in Miami — Cesly has always had a passion for writing. As she honed in on her calling and intentionally listened to God, she came to understand that engaging blog/social posts and freelance content were only the beginning. Christian Singles were her calling. Going through the trenches of dating woes were her assignment. But what many assumed was for her harm, God chose to use for the good — so that many may be saved from the heartache and stress that Dating With*out* Dignity can cause. A graduate of the University of Central Florida, a certified Empowerment Coach, and thanks to all that this journey has taught her, your Single Life Liaison — Cesly has accepted her mission to boldly walk and share the lessons learned from any aspect of her life that seems fit.

Today, Cesly resides in Atlanta, GA where she is continually working on her craft, sharing her talents, and following the calling on her life — which is to ultimately live it to the fullest...unapologetically.

www.ingramcontent.com/pod-product-compliance
Lightning Source LLC
Chambersburg PA
CBHW022035090426
42741CB00007B/1079